DICKENS (ABRIDGED)

Adam Long

BROADWAY PLAY PUBLISHING INC
New York
www.broadwayplaypublishing.com
info@broadwayplaypublishing.com

First printing: July 2011
Second printing: February 2012
I S B N: 978-0-88145-448-2

Book design: Marie Donovan
Page make-up: Adobe Indesign
Typeface: Palatino
Printed and bound in the U S A

ABOUT THE AUTHOR

Adam Long was a founding member/writer/
director of the Reduced Shakespeare Company. THE
COMPLETE WORKS OF WILLIAM SHAKESPEARE
(ABRIDGED), which Adam directed and co-wrote,
ran in London's West End for nine years and was
nominated for an Olivier Award. SHAKESPEARE
(ABRIDGED) also ran Off-Broadway twice and
continues to enjoy numerous successful tours
throughout the world.

In 2003, his feature-length film *The Barn* won The
Raindance Award at the British Independent Film
Awards. Adam has written for Disney Channel
(*History on Toast* and *Last Minute Book Reports*), P B S
(*The Complete Works of William Shakespeare (abridged)*),
B B C One (*Rolf on Art*), Channel Four (*Trigger Happy
T V* and *The Ring Reduced*), B B C Radio Four
(*Condensed Histories* and *Home Truths*) and Lucasfilm
& BSkyB (*Star Wars Shortened*). Other stage shows
include THE BIBLE: THE COMPLETE WORD OF
GOD (abridged) and THE COMPLETE HISTORY
OF AMERICA (abridged) (Reduced Shakespeare
Company); and DECONSTRUCTING ALBERT (The
Crucible Theatre, Sheffield).

DICKENS (ABRIDGED) was developed and produced in the U K under the title DICKENS UNPLUGGED. It was first performed in the Assembly Rooms during the 2007 Edinburgh Fringe Festival. The cast was as follows:

Luke Evans
Matthew Hendrickson
Simon Jermond
Bryan Torfeh
Gabriel Vick

DICKENS (ABRIDGED) then played at the Yvonne Arnaud Theatre in Guildford. The cast was as follows:

Joseph Attenborough
Matthew Hendrickson
Simon Jermond
Jon Robyns
Gabriel Vick

DICKENS (ABRIDGED) was produced at The Comedy Theatre in London in 2008. The cast was as follows:

Joseph Attenborough
Matthew Hendrickson
Simon Jermond
Adam Long
Gabriel Vick
Ben Heathcote (cover)
Bryan Torfeh (cover)

All three U K productions featured a cast of five actor/ musicians playing multiple roles. This version of the script reflects the casting of the production mounted in London. So, for example, ADAM as SCROOGE bears the heading SCROOGE/ADAM. However, this is intended as a casting guideline. If the talents of your acting company dictate that parts are assigned differently to make your particular production work, feel free to do so. Likewise with the musical arrangement—the music can be arranged to best suit the skills of your performers.

ASSIGNMENT OF ROLES (LONDON):

Joseph Attenborough *(guitar, double bass, banjolele, piano, accordion)* OLIVER TWIST, WILLIAM HALL, DAVID COPPERFIELD, MISS HAVISHAM, MADAME DEFARGE, CHARLES DARNAY, BOB CRATCHIT, THE GHOST OF CHRISTMAS PAST, *and others.*

Matthew Hendrickson *(percussion, accordion)* MR SOWERBERRY, NANCY, MR WARREN, MR MURDSTONE, TRADDLES, MR MICAWBER, MR PEGGOTTY, LUCIE MANETTE, THE GHOST OF CHRISTMAS PRESENT, *and others.*

Simon Jermond *(guitar, electric crutch, trumpet)* THE ARTFUL DODGER, BARKIS, AGNES WICKFIELD, URIAH HEEP, CATHERINE DICKENS, DR MANETTE, TINY TIM, THE GHOST OF CHRISTMAS YET TO COME, *and others.*

Adam Long *(guitar, piano, harmonica)* BEADLE BUMBLE, FAGIN, CLARA COPPERFIELD, MR CREAKLE, DORA SPENLOW, ELLEN TERNAN, SYDNEY CARTON, EBENEZER SCROOGE, *and others.*

Gabriel Vick *(guitar, piano, trumpet)* CHARLES DICKENS, CLARA PEGGOTTY, JAMES STEERFORTH, BETSEY TROTWOOD, MRS CRATCHIT, *and others*

Many thanks to the following people for their prodigious talents, contributions to the script, and overall development of the production: Joseph Attenborough, Luke Evans, Ben Heathcote, Matthew Hendrickson, Alex Jackson-Long, Simon Jermond, Jon Robyns, Giles Terera, Bryan Torfeh, and Gabriel Vick. And, of course, thanks to Charles Dickens for being the greatest author in the history of the universe.

ACT ONE

(The stage is mostly empty except for an easel with a sign that reads DICKENS ABRIDGED *to one side.)*

(There are a couple of wooden crates that will be used as stools.)

(There is one rack of costumes.)

(There is an upright piano.)

(Houselights are still up and the stage remains in pre-set as ADAM, JOSEPH, MATTHEW, *and* SIMON *come onto the stage one by one, informally—some of them enter from wings, some enter from audience. They are carrying more props and costumes and placing them around the stage in preparation for the start of the show.)*

(As they speak, they speak quietly, naturally—not as if they expect the audience to hear [unless they are speaking directly to them]).

(The actors are just in contemporary clothes—they look as if they could be stagehands. But as they set up the stage, they also put on bits and pieces of Victorian costume, so by the end of the scene they all look completely Dickensian.)

ADAM: *(To audience)* Don't stop talking. This isn't the show yet. *(To* SIMON*)* It's good to see there are so many Dickens lovers in *(Insert name of town).*

SIMON: I know.

MATTHEW: Where do these go?

(MATTHEW *and* JOSEPH *are pushing a rack of costumes.*)

ADAM: Over there.

SIMON: *(To audience member)* Would you hold this for me? *(He hands a sign to the audience member, then hammers a nail into the proscenium. Takes the sign back from the audience member)* Thanks. *(He hangs the sign up. It says* THE FEZZIWIGS IN CONCERT.*)*

JOSEPH: Who's got the set list?

ADAM: *(Handing him a paper with a list of songs in magic marker)* Here.

JOSEPH: Can we tape this down here?

ADAM: That's good for me.

SIMON: Go for it.

(JOSEPH *pulls out some duct tape and starts taping the list to the stage floor. The list, handwritten with magic marker, reads:*)

CHARLIE DICKENS
OLIVER TWISTED
CHARLIE REPRISE
MR WARREN/FAMOUS WRITER
BLEAK HOUSE
ANXIETY AND SORROW
AGNES LAMENT
WEDDING MARCH
GREAT EXPECTATIONS
DAVID COPPERFIELD EPILOGUE
MYSTERY SONG
LULLABY/DEMENTIA
FOOTSTEPS
FAR FAR BETTER
CURIOSITY SHOP
GRAVE
TINY TIM

TINY TIM REPRISE
FINALE

(Meanwhile, MATTHEW *is testing the microphones [if there are any] by tapping them.)*

JOSEPH: *(Looking at the set list)* Oh man, we're not doing Oliver Twist tonight are we?!?

ADAM: We're totally doing Oliver Twist.

JOSEPH: I hate that. It's all singing and dancing—it's total cheesefest.

ADAM: We can't cut Oliver Twist—people love Oliver Twist.

SIMON: I love the end where Fagin and the Dodger skip off arm in arm. That's my favorite—I love that.

MATTHEW: That's only in the movie. In the book Fagin dies. He gets hung by the neck. He goes all insane. It's really dark.

SIMON: I knew that.

JOSEPH: *(To* SIMON*)* You never even read the book I bet.

SIMON: Whatever.

JOSEPH: That's very mature.

SIMON: Whatever.

MATTHEW: I hate it when he does that.

JOSEPH: I don't want to do Oliver.

ADAM: We're doing Oliver. Let's take a vote... *(To audience)* How many of you want to see Oliver?

(The audience raises their hands.)

ADAM: There. We're doing Oliver.

JOSEPH: Oliver sucks.

ADAM: Shut up man. The only reason we let you in this group was because you had a van.

(MATTHEW *is sweeping the stage.*)

MATTHEW: God, this stage is filthy. What was on here before us?

SIMON: I think it was (*Insert name of show from the night before, or perhaps an event that happened in the theatre during the day*).

MATTHEW: I wish they'd cleaned up after themselves.

(SIMON *has been tuning his guitar. He strums a few cords.*)

SIMON: Okay you guys. I'm ready.

ADAM: You're ready?

SIMON: Yeah.

ADAM: Okay, let's go for it.

(ADAM, JOSEPH, *and* MATTHEW *exit, leaving* SIMON, *dressed as the Artful Dodger, alone on the stage.*)

(*The houselights dim, the stage lights rise.*)

(SIMON, *dressed as the Artful Dodger, sings soulfully.*)

Song: **The Ballad Of Charles Dickens**

SIMON:
Charlie Dickens walked the streets of London town
Like a colossus Charlie Dickens strode
At daybreak he would hit the lanes of Clerkenwell
By ten fifteen he'd be on Old King's Road

(JOSEPH *enters from the wings and harmonizes with* SIMON.)

SIMON & JOSEPH:
Charlie Dickens walked the streets and never stopped
His elbows rubbed with beggars thieves and whores
The great black dome of old Saint Paul's looked down
  on him
The smell of death creeped from the river's shore

(ADAM *enters strumming a second guitar. They sing in three-part harmony.*)

SIMON, JOSEPH, & ADAM;
All the way from Camden
To Shoreditch he would roam
Down streets asmear with slaughtered pigs
With fat and blood and foam
He'd drink some beer
Eat lunch and then go home

(MATTHEW *enters with a triangle, rings it on the beat, and exits again.*)

ADAM:
There was a London town of old
In Charlie Dickens' boyhood dream

JOSEPH:
And then there was a London town
Of industry, of smoke and steam

SIMON:
Between the two a lonesome road
Upon which Charlie Dickens strode

(MATTHEW *re-enters and joins the singing.*)

ALL:
Charlie Dickens walked the streets
Charlie Dickens walked the streets
Charlie Dickens walked the streets
Of London town

ADAM: (*To audience*) Ladies and Gentlemen, the great man himself...Mister Charles Dickens!

(*The boys lead wild applause.*)

(*Lights up as* CHARLES DICKENS *[GABE] enters. He shakes hands with the cast and with a few audience members.*)

JOSEPH: Charles Dickens, everybody!! Check it out!!!

SIMON: The man! The man!

DICKENS/GABE: Thank you. Thank you ladies and gentlemen. Thank you very much. Please. Shut up ladies and gentlemen. My name is Charles Dickens, and this is the band—boys, do you want to introduce yourselves?

ADAM: Yeah. The name of this band is The Fezziwigs, okay? We're from Santa Cruz California *(Or insert name of hometown here)* —we're actually the biggest Charles Dickens tribute band in Santa Cruz *(Or hometown)*. And we're here tonight to pay tribute to the life and works of the greatest man who ever lived! Boom!

(DICKENS raises his hand. ADAM gives him a high five.)

DICKENS/GABE: Well said! *(To audience)* Now I'm sure that most of you are familiar with my work, so I'm not about to boast about the fact that I wrote sixty-one works of fiction and non-fiction, or that I was a major influence on great thinkers such as Karl Marx and Sigmund Freud, and I certainly don't feel we need to dwell on the work I did for charity. I am simply here to thank you for coming, and to say that in the next ninety minutes, you are about to see something incredibly special—the life and works of me, Charles Dickens. I'd like to begin by posing a question—why?

(Special on DICKENS and SIMON. The others exit.)

(SIMON plays an atmospheric guitar arpeggio beneath.)

DICKENS/GABE: Why is there cruelty and greed?

SIMON: *(Singing)*
Charlie saw poor orphans who had lost all hope

DICKENS/GABE: *(Spoken)* Why are the most vulnerable the most abused?

SIMON: *(Singing)*
In huddled filth behind the workhouse gate

DICKENS/GABE: *(Spoken)* What is the root of man's inhumanity to man?

SIMON: *(Singing)*
Charlie Dickens vowed that he would tell the world

DICKENS/GABE: *(Spoken)* Who will be the voice of the oppressed and downtrodden?

SIMON: *(Singing)*
Pay heed good folk to these poor children's fate

DICKENS/GABE: *(Spoken)* Consider the workhouse—a living grave for the unwanted, the unloved, the poor and the hopeless; The workhouse—where mere children were left to die by a gradual process of neglect and starvation. Ladies and Gentlemen, this is the story of Oliver Twist.

(SIMON reveals a sign reading OLIVER TWIST.)

(Lights up on JOSEPH [dressed as OLIVER] and MATTHEW [dressed as a workhouse URCHIN]. They carry bowls and spoons, and strike a dramatic pose.)

OLIVER/JOSEPH & URCHIN/MATTHEW: Ya-da-da-da-da-da! Oh—

(Lights up bright. Suddenly, OLIVER and the URCHIN are dancing, smiling, and high-kicking!)

Song: **Oliver With A Twist**

OLIVER/JOSEPH & URCHIN/MATTHEW:
Gruel
Gruel
Marvelous gruel
It's the only thing that keeps us
From death's door
Gruel
Gruel
Wonderous gruel
Marvelous

Wonderous
Fabulous
Good for us...

(MATTHEW *exits.* ADAM *enters dressed as* BEADLE.)

OLIVER/JOSEPH: *(Spoken)* Please sir, I want some more.

BEADLE/ADAM: More!?!
Oliver Twist
Stop your yelping
Nobody gets
A second helping
Oliver Twist
Let me tell ya
Time has come
For me to sell ya

(*Enter* MATTHEW *as an* UNDERTAKER.)

BEADLE/ADAM: Who will buy this boyyyyyyy!!!!

UNDERTAKER/MATTHEW: *(Spoken)* I'll take him.

BEADLE/ADAM: Sold!

(UNDERTAKER *and* BEADLE *shake hands and exit.*)

(*Lights shift to a special on* OLIVER.)

OLIVER/JOSEPH: *(Sung)* Whe-e-e-e-ere is lunch

(SIMON *[dressed as the* DODGER*] joins* JOSEPH *in the special.*)

DODGER/SIMON: *(Spoken)* Welcome to London, where life is jolly and everyone dances, even the butchers and whores.

OLIVER/JOSEPH: My name is Oliver Twist and I've come to London to seek my fortune.

DODGER/SIMON: I'm the Artful Dodger. Would you like to come live with a good-hearted Jew who's got a thing for little boys?

OLIVER/JOSEPH: You bet I would!

DODGER/SIMON: *(Sung)* I consider you to be my friend
For I immediately comprehend

(Lights full up. MATTHEW, dressed as a butcher, with a bloody apron and cap, and carrying a large slab of meat, joins SIMON and JOSEPH. The three of them form a chorus line.)

ALL:
That you're the kinda boy on whom we can depend
We consider you to be our friend

(Exit MATTHEW. Enter ADAM dressed as FAGIN.)

FAGIN/ADAM: If I were a rich man
Deegle deegle deegle
(Spoken) Oh hello. Who's this, then?

DODGER/SIMON: This is Oliver Twist.

OLIVER/JOSEPH: I've come to London to seek my fortune.

FAGIN/ADAM: Well, Oliver... *(Sung:)*
You will never come to grief, boy
If you learn to be a thief, oy!

ALL: Who will I be robbing this morning
Who will I be robbing today

(Enter MATTHEW dressed as NANCY in a red dress and carrying a club.)

NANCY/MATTHEW: As long as he beats me

(NANCY smashes herself three times on the head [on words "he", "beats" and "me"]. Cymbal crash as club hits her.)

DODGER/SIMON: Oliver, this is Nancy—and I'd do anything for her.

OLIVER/LUKE: *(To NANCY)* Will you be my mommy and live with us happily ever after?

NANCY/MATTHEW: Sorry boys, I've got to get bludgeoned to death.

ALL: *(Disappointed)* Awwww.

NANCY/MATTHEW: But the good news is that Oliver's going to be adopted by his rich uncle!!!

ALL: Hooray!!!
Yes you're the kinda boy
On whom we can depend
We consider you
Sider you
Sider you to be our friend...hey!

(Bows and wild applause)

(Blackout)

*(*MATTHEW *exits, removing the* OLIVER TWIST *sign as he goes.)*

(Lights up: a special on SIMON, *who is joined by* ADAM *and* JOSEPH. *All three play guitar.)*

Song: **Ballad Of Charles Dickens Reprise 1**

SIMON, ADAM & JOSEPH:
Charlie Dickens' father fell to poverty
He went to prison down in Marshalsea
Charlie was a boy when he was sent to work
In Mister Warren's blacking factory

(They exit except ADAM.)

ADAM: *(To audience)* 1824—Near the Hungerford Stairs, young Charles Dickens, only twelve years old, toils relentlessly in Warren's Boot Blacking Factory. *(He exits.)*

(Lights shift to reveal a sign reading WARREN'S BOOT BLACKING—MANUFACTURED BY REAL CHILDREN.)

(Lights up on DICKENS, *dressed as a dirty 12 year old boy. He is dragging a large sack labelled* COAL *across the stage. He is walking on his knees to make himself seem small.)*

(Enter MATTHEW *dressed as* MR WARREN, *the factory owner. He carries two megaphones—old fashion style megaphones, not electric ones. His costume will need to be distinctive so he can be easily recognised when he returns in* ACT TWO.*)*

MR WARREN/MATTHEW: *(Through megaphone)* Hello Charles!

DICKENS/GABE: *(Startled)* Aaaa! Oh Mister Warren.

MR WARREN/MATTHEW: Didn't mean to frighten you. I was just testing out these megaphones. They'll be ideal for terrorizing the nine year-olds on the shop floor.

DICKENS/GABE: I didn't know you were there.

MR WARREN/MATTHEW: *(Cheerful)* I wanted to see how you were getting on.

DICKENS/GABE: Well, I was filling bottles this morning like you asked me...

MR WARREN/MATTHEW: Good.

DICKENS/GABE: But I'm afraid there was a bit of a hitch.

MR WARREN/MATTHEW: Oh dear.

DICKENS/GABE: Little Mick Jones got his hair caught in the machinery, and I had to take a break while we searched for his head.

MR WARREN/MATTHEW: No need to apologize. You are a dedicated young man, Charles. I applaud that. How do you like your new location? I thought you'd like being by the window?

DICKENS/GABE: I know you mean well, Mister Warren, but I really don't like being by the window. People look at me and laugh because I'm a poor young boy working in a factory.

MR WARREN/MATTHEW: You should never be ashamed of filling blacking bottles, Charles. It's a noble job, and you do it well. In time, you could move on to labelling.

DICKENS/GABE: Mister Warren, I've had a letter.
(Produces a tattered letter)

MR WARREN/MATTHEW: A letter?

(DICKENS shows the letter to MR WARREN.)

DICKENS/GABE: It's from my father. His release date has come up—at the end of the month. He'll be getting out of debtors prison and I'll be going home.

MR WARREN/MATTHEW: No, don't be silly, Charles, you don't have to go home. You could stay here at the factory. You're a good worker and I'd be proud to keep you on.

DICKENS/GABE: No, Mr. Warren, I'm leaving at the end of the month.

MR WARREN/MATTHEW: I'll move you away from the window.

DICKENS/GABE: It's not about the window! I want to go back to school. I want to be a writer.

MR WARREN/MATTHEW: Why would you want to be a writer when you could work in a factory? You're happy here, aren't you?

DICKENS/GABE: No, Mister Warren! I'm not happy here! I—I don't like blacking, Mister Warren!

(Beat)

(MR WARREN is visibly heartbroken.)

MR WARREN/MATTHEW: You don't like blacking? How long have you felt this way?

DICKENS/GABE: I've always felt this way. The thought, smell and appearance of blacking arouses anxieties and sorrows within me.

MR WARREN/MATTHEW: Anxieties and sorrows?

DICKENS/GABE: I'm sorry.

MR WARREN/MATTHEW: No, I'm sorry. People warned me—they said you were just using me while your family was in prison. But I said, "No! Charles is different!" I should have listened.

DICKENS/GABE: Look, let's try to make the best of it till the end of the month—

MR WARREN/MATTHEW: Why wait till the end of the month?!? Why don't you go now!

DICKENS/GABE: Where will I go?

MR WARREN/MATTHEW: Live on the street with the urchins and pickpockets for all I care!

DICKENS/GABE: That's not fair!

MR WARREN/MATTHEW: Don't talk to me about fair! Just go! Now!

DICKENS/GABE: Alright. If that's the way you want it. *(He stands up)*

I came in here a child, but I'm walking out a man. Mark my words, Mister Warren, one day I'm going to write great stories about how poor children are mistreated by men like you. And my stories are going to change the world!

MR WARREN/MATTHEW: If you'll excuse me—I've got some blacking to manufacture!

DICKENS/GABE: Good bye, Mister Warren. Good bye forever!

(DICKENS heads for the door, but MR WARREN stops him by shouting through the megaphone.)

MR WARREN/MATTHEW: *(Through megaphone)* Wait... Charles...

DICKENS/GABE: What!

(ADAM *plays an arpeggio on the guitar.*)

Song: **So Long**

MR WARREN/MATTHEW:
This factory could be your home
If only you would let it

DICKENS/GABE: *(Spoken)* No, Mister Warren, I could
never be happy here.

MR WARREN/MATTHEW:
If you walk out that door today
Tomorrow you'll regret it

DICKENS/GABE: *(Spoken)* Aw shucks, Mister Warren...
you're breakin' my heart! *(Sung:)*
I've got to go
And there aint no use cryin'
Each day I stay
There's a part of me dyin'
We both know that in my heart
There is something lacking
I do believe there's more to life
Than filling bottles up with blacking

BOTH: *(Harmonizing through megaphones)*
Things will never be the same
Once you [I] are [am] gone
The time has come to say 'so long'

(MATTHEW *exits.*)

(*Lights shift.* DICKENS *dances happily across the stage
changing into more grown-up clothing and picking up a
briefcase along the way.*)

(ADAM *and* SIMON *play an upbeat vamp on guitars.*)

Song: **Aint Goin Back To Blacking**

DICKENS/GABE: A famous writer
Is what I'm gonna be
I'm gonna feed the hungry
And set the poor people free
And I aint goin back
To that blacking fac-to-ry

ADAM & SIMON:
A famous writer
Is what he's gonna be

DICKENS/GABE: Oh yes I am! I'm gonna write some novels!

ADAM & SIMON:
He's gonna feed the hungry
And set the poor people free

DICKENS/GABE: Work for charity! And edit periodicals!

ALL: And he aint goin back
To that blacking
Fac-to-

(DICKENS *mimes knocking on a door.)*

(JOSEPH, *dressed as* WILLIAM HALL *the publisher, mimes opening a door.)*

HALL/JOSEPH: What!

DICKENS/GABE: Are you Mr. William Hall, the highly successful publisher?

HALL/JOSEPH: Who the hell are you?

DICKENS/GABE: I'm Charles Dickens. One day I'm going to be a great author and I want you to publish my works.

HALL/JOSEPH: Wannabe authors are a dime a dozen, Dickens! Now get out!

DICKENS/GABE: I'm not leaving here until you give me a publishing deal—and believe me there is NO WAY I'm going back to work in a blacking factory!

HALL/JOSEPH: Who said anything about working in a blacking factory?!? Are you some kind of lunatic?!?

DICKENS/GABE: Yes I am! Have you got a problem with that!?

(Beat, as two stand nose to nose.)

(HALL smiles and laughs.)

HALL/JOSEPH: Dickens, I like your spirit. I've been looking for someone to do episodic fiction—lighthearted, but with an element of social critique.

(DICKENS scribbles madly in his notebook, rips out the page and hands it to HALL.)

DICKENS/GABE: Here's your first episode. I call it Pickwick Papers.

HALL/JOSEPH: *(Shouting offstage)* Boy!

(A newspaper delivery BOY enters. HALL hands him the page.)

BOY/SIMON: Yes sir!

HALL/JOSEPH: Get this out on the street! Let's see what the public have to say.

(BOY steps outside and begins hawking his page.)

(MATTHEW and ADAM enter as members of the public.)

BOY/SIMON: Extra! Extra! Read all about it! First episode of *Pickwick Papers*, by Charles Dickens, unknown author!

(MATTHEW and ADAM struggle with one another to buy the page.)

PUBLIC 1/MATTHEW: I'll take it!

PUBLIC 2/ADAM: No me! Let me read it!

PUBLIC 1/MATTHEW: *(Reading the page)* Oh my, that's fantastic! It's funny and it brought a tear to my eye.

PUBLIC 2/ADAM: *(Reading over his shoulder)* It's like he looked into our homes and wrote exactly what he saw!

PUBLIC 1/MATTHEW: I can't wait till the next episode!

PUBLIC 2/ADAM: Me neither!

(They exit.)

HALL/JOSEPH: Well Dickens, you're a hit!

DICKENS/GABE: Yes!

HALL/JOSEPH: I want one of these every month!

DICKENS/GABE: You got it!

HALL/JOSEPH: Dickens, this is the beginning of something big. You stick with me and you'll be rich and famous—and you'll never have to work in that blacking factory again!

(ADAM and SIMON vamp on guitars.)

(HALL exits.)

DICKENS/GABE: Yee haw!!

Song: **Aint Goin Back To Blacking (Reprise)**

DICKENS/GABE:
Oh I love to write
And my public they love me

ADAM & SIMON:
The public love him
They really really love him

DICKENS/GABE: Episodic fiction
Sets my spirit free

ADAM & SIMON:
It's episodic
Published on a monthly basis

DICKENS/GABE: And I aint goin back
To that blacking
Fac-to—

(*Lights and music shift abruptly.* DICKENS *stands in a special, gazing into the distance.*)

DICKENS/GABE: Unlimited...
My future is unlimited

(*Lights and music shift back.*)

ALL: And I aint goin back
To that blacking
Fac-to-ry
No I aint goin back
To that blacking
Fac-to-ry
The blacking factory

(*Blackout*)

(*Special on* MATTHEW *standing beside easel.*)

MATTHEW: And now, we are proud to present that heartbreaking tale of love and mystery—ladies and gentlemen, *Bleak House.*

(MATTHEW *reveals a sign reading* BLEAK HOUSE, *and exits.*)

(*Lights up*)

(SIMON *schlepps across the stage with his guitar. He looks at the sign, thinks about it a second, and then launches into a song.*)

Song: **Bleak House**

SIMON: Oh Lady Dedlock had a bastard girl
Out of wedlock born
And she had a shifty lawyer
By the name of Tulkinghorn
And she asked him to keep mum

And he told her where to get off
Then Hortense got a gun
And blew his head off
Then Richard kicks the bucket
And everything gets gnarly
When Jo comes down with smallpox
And he passes it to Charley
But there's a happy ending
Because Esther finds a spouse
And that is the story of *Bleak House*
(Spoken) Thank you.

(Applause)

(SIMON reveals a sign that reads DAVID COPPERFIELD and exits.)

(Enter JOSEPH dressed as DAVID COPPERFIELD as a boy. DAVID has distinctive curly hair.)

DAVID/JOSEPH: My name is David Copperfield. My father died before I was born, and my mother married a violent psychopath named Murdstone.

(Enter ADAM as DAVID's MOTHER, and MATTHEW as MR MURDSTONE—dressed in black with distinctive moustache.)

DAVID/JOSEPH: Then mama gave birth a baby boy...

(MOTHER holds up an infant with a black moustache.)

DAVID/JOSEPH: ...and Murdstone kept trying to beat me every five minutes, so I bit his hand.

(MURDSTONE points at DAVID.)

(During the lines below, DAVID mimes biting his hand. MURDSTONE mimes slamming and locking a door. DAVID mimes pounding on the door.)

DAVID/JOSEPH: Chomp.

MURDSTONE/MATTHEW: Aaa! Slam. Lock. Kerchink. Click.

DAVID/JOSEPH: Thump. Thump. Thump. I was locked in my room, then sent away to boarding school. I said goodbye to my nurse, Peggotty

(A suitcase is thrown to DAVID from the wings.)

(PEGGOTTY [GABE in a fat suit] runs hysterically to DAVID and buries his face in her bosom.)

PEGGOTTY/GABE: Oh Davy, I can't bear to see you go! Let me hold you to my heaving bosom! Let me look at you! I can't look at you! Oh flail! Flail! Flail!

(During the above, BARKIS [SIMON], enters and watches.)

(PEGGOTTY exits, flailing wildly.)

BARKIS/SIMON: That maid of yours is hot. You tell her; Barkis is willing!

(BARKIS trots at a leisurely pace towards the wings. A clip-clop noise on cocoanuts approximates the sound of horse hooves. BARKIS disappears into the wings.)

DAVID/JOSEPH: At school I met my first true friend.

(Enter GABE as STEERFORTH and MATTHEW as TRADDLES. STEERFORTH strides over to DAVID and shakes his hand.)

STEERFORTH/GABE: Welcome to Mister Creakle's boarding school. I'm James Steerforth, head boy.

(They shake hands.)

DAVID/JOSEPH: God you're handsome and dashing. I'm utterly in love with you already. My name is David Copperfield, but you can call me "Davy".

STEERFORTH/GABE: Very well, Daisy. Will you tell me stories at bedtime?

(Enter TRADDLES. He has absurd hair that stands straight up.)

DAVID/JOSEPH: You bet I will.

TRADDLES/MATTHEW: Oh hello. My name is Traddles.

DAVID/JOSEPH: My name is David Copperfield.

TRADDLES/MATTHEW: How capital to meet you. I have a feeling we're going to be friends for the rest of our lives.

DAVID/JOSEPH: Yeah, whatever...so Steerforth, old buddy, what time do you want me in your room for the storytelling?

STEERFORTH/GABE: Sixish, I suppose, Daisy.

TRADDLES/MATTHEW: Heads up lads, here comes Mister Creakle!

(MR CREAKLE *enters and beats* DAVID *across the back three times with his cane.*)

MR CREAKLE/ADAM: Thwack!

DAVID/JOSEPH: Aaaa!

MR CREAKLE/ADAM: Thwack!

DAVID/JOSEPH: Aaaa!

MR CREAKLE/ADAM: Thwack!

DAVID/JOSEPH: Aaaa! Why did you do that, sir?

MR CREAKLE/ADAM: I don't even know. (*To audience*) I should be in prison.

(STEERFORTH *and* TRADDLES *exit.*)

MR CREAKLE/ADAM: Master Copperfield, I'm afraid I've got some bad news for you—Your mother and brother are dead.

(MR CREAKLE *plays an ominous chord on the piano.*)

(*Lights up on a tombstone reading* HERE LIES DAVID COPPERFIELD'S WHOLE FAMILY.)

(MR CREAKLE *plays atmospheric chords beneath.*)

DAVID/JOSEPH: My mother and brother dead?!? Now I'm an orphan, and I just know Mister Murdstone is going to send me to work in a bleak warehouse and

I'll end up running away in a desperate search for my
eccentric Aunt Betsey. Oh misery! Misery! Did ever a
young boy suffer under the weight of such oppressive
melancholy and despair? Who is the architect of such
calamity? Who would do such terrible things to an
innocent child?

(DAVID *and* MR CREAKLE *exit.*)

(*Enter* DICKENS *[*GABE*] with a pen in one hand and paper
in the other. The paper is on a hand held writing desk,
similar to a painter's pallet.*)

(SIMON, *dressed as* URIAH HEEP *plays guitar.*)

Song: **Anxiety And Sorrow**

DICKENS/GABE: With this pen
And this piece of paper
I make women cry
And grown men weep
With this pen
I killed David Copperfield's mother
And sent his baby brother to eternal sleep
With this pen
I can give you hope today
But I'll take it away again
Tomorrow
I am a man
Of anxiety and sorrow

(*Enter* MATTHEW *as* MR MICAWBER.)

MICAWBER/MATTHEW: With that pen
He set me to debtors jail
Locked me up like a dirty robber
I am a man of talent
Waiting for something to turn up
My name is Wilkins Micawber
Hey mister landlord
Won't you take my I O U

And do you have some cash
That I can borrow

BOTH: I am a man
Of anxiety and sorrow

MICAWBER/MATTHEW: You gave me no money

DICKENS/GABE: I gave you life

MICAWBER/MATTHEW: You gave me no job

DICKENS/GABE: I gave you a wife

MICAWBER/MATTHEW: You gave me in-laws
Who think I'm a slob

DICKENS/GABE: I did that for comic effect

MICAWBER/MATTHEW: You made me wretched
Oh You made me weep

DICKENS/GABE: It could have been worse
You could have been Uriah Heep

(Dramatic shift in lighting as URIAH HEEP *[*SIMON*] strides forward.)*

HEEP/SIMON:
I am a man
Whose name is Uriah
I tell you that I'm umble
But you know I'm a liar
I'm a heep of infamy
A social pariah
I rub my hands
Because my palms perspire
Hey Mister Dickens
Tell me why for pity sake
You made me a cross
Between a fish and a snake

(Enter DAVID.*)*

DAVID/JOSEPH: You made me an orphan

HEEP/SIMON: You made me corrupt

[JOSEPH: I wish I'd never been born]

MICAWBER/MATTHEW: Mister Dickens
You made me
A lovable bankrupt

[JOSEPH: What is your problem? Why are you so mis'rable and hollow?]

HEEP/SIMON & MICAWBER/MATTHEW:
Why did you create me
To live a life so mis'rable
And hollow

DICKENS/GABE: Because I
Am a man
Of anxiety and sorrow

ALL: I am a man
Of anxiety and sorrow

(Black out)

(Lights up on MATTHEW.*)*

MATTHEW: In 1855, Charles Dickens wrote one of his most trenchant works, meditating on prison as a metaphor representing the constraints and inhibitions of Victorian society, and the rigid bonds inherent in the class system. Ladies and gentlemen, we are proud to present Dickens' subtle and complex tale of love and retribution...*Little Dorrit.*

*(*MATTHEW *reveals a sign reading* LITTLE DORRIT *and exits.)*

*(*SIMON *enters carrying a scrap of paper. He ambles over to the sign, looks at it, then refers to his scrap of paper.)*

SIMON: *(Reading)* "There once was a young girl named Dorrit. If your dress had a rip she'd restore it. When she was importuned to claim a large fortune she thought it was best to ignore it." Thank you.

(SIMON *exits, revealing a sign reading* AND NOW BACK
TO DAVID COPPERFIELD.)

(*Lights up on* DAVID *as an adult, still with the distinctive
curly hair.*)

DAVID/JOSEPH: At this point, many years passed
quickly.

(GABE *runs across the stage carrying a sign that reads*
MANY YEARS.)

DAVID/JOSEPH: I became a young man and moved to
London to seek my fortune. One day there was a knock
on my door.

(SIMON *dressed as* AGNES *enters carrying a door. He sets
it on the stage, knocks on it, and then walks around it to
approach* DAVID.)

DAVID/JOSEPH: Oh, hello Agnes—my dearest, pure-
hearted childhood friend.

AGNES/SIMON: David, I'm here to warn you that your
school friend, Steerforth, is morally unsound.

DAVID/JOSEPH: Agnes, you are beautiful and saintly
and I love you like a sister, and you may be right about
Steerforth. But let me tell you this—you're wrong
about Steerforth.

(AGNES *exits.*)

(MR PEGGOTTY [MATTHEW], *a sailor dressed in heavy
weather gear, enters. He knocks on the door.*)

DAVID/JOSEPH: Come in. Why it's Mister Peggotty,
the seafaring brother of my nurse, and guardian to the
enchanting Little Emily who is engaged to be married
to his nephew Ham!

MR PEGGOTTY/MATTHEW: Oh Mas'r Davy! Have you
seen 'er?

DAVID/JOSEPH: Who?

MR PEGGOTTY/MATTHEW: Little Emily! She's run off
with that villainous Steerforth, and I just know he's
going to take her to Europe and abandon her to a life of
prostitution! *(He exits.)*

(AGNES knocks on the door and re-enters.)

DAVID/JOSEPH: Agnes!

AGNES/SIMON: Yeah?

DAVID/JOSEPH: Do you remember what you said about
Steerforth?

AGNES/SIMON: That he's morally unsound?

DAVID/JOSEPH: It turns out you were totally right.
He destroys the lives of common people and thinks
nothing of it.

AGNES/SIMON: I won't say "I told you so".

DAVID/JOSEPH: I still love him, though.

AGNES/SIMON: Of course.

DAVID/JOSEPH: Listen, I'm glad you're here. My
dearest Agnes, I want to confide something to you.

AGNES/SIMON: Yes Davy?

DAVID/JOSEPH: It is...an affair of the heart.

AGNES/SIMON: An affair of the heart?

*(DAVID pulls up two crates to be used as stools. DAVID and
AGNES sit down together. DAVID holds her hand in his.)*

DAVID/JOSEPH: There is someone who I have cared
about deeply for some time—someone who I intend to
ask to be my wife.

AGNES/SIMON: *(Eagerly)* Who?

DAVID/JOSEPH: Dora Spenlow, the charming airhead
daughter of my tight-fisted employer.

AGNES/SIMON: *(Taken aback)* Oh...Dora...I see...and
she's an airhead you say?

DAVID/JOSEPH: As thick as a plank.

AGNES/SIMON: Well that's good. That's good.

DAVID/JOSEPH: Do you really think so?

AGNES/SIMON: Yes, yes—who wants to marry a woman of intelligence.

DAVID/JOSEPH: Exactly! Oh Agnes, I just had to confide in you because I think of you as my dearest sister.

AGNES/SIMON: Thank you. I'm very happy for you.

DAVID/JOSEPH: You are?

AGNES/SIMON: Yes.

DAVID/JOSEPH: You don't seem very happy.

AGNES/SIMON: Well, I've got a lot on my mind, what with father's alcoholism and Uriah Heep's blackmail... but I am happy for you, very.

DAVID/JOSEPH: Oh Agnes, you are a saint! Pointing me always upward! I must go! Farewell.

AGNES/SIMON: Farewell Davy.

(DAVID *happily exits.*)

AGNES/SIMON: *(Under breath)* What an asshole.

(GABE *and* MATTHEW *enter as blind men, wearing round dark glasses.* GABE *plays guitar. Note:* MATTHEW *is underdressed as* VICAR.)

Song: **Agnes Lament**

AGNES/SIMON:
My name is Agnes and my tale is sad
Davy was the only true love I ever had
But love is blind and Cupid is a trickster
Davy only loves me like a saint or like a sister

AGNES & BLINDMEN:
Oh Davy, Davy
I'm the truest love you'll ever find

Oh Davy boy
Why are you blind blind blind?

AGNES/SIMON: He tells me he loves Dora
And she will be his bride
I wanna rip her head off
But I keep it all inside
Dora's cute and curly
With a head like a bubble
She talks just like a baby
I wanna smack her with a shovel

AGNES & BLINDMEN
Oh Davy, Davy
I'm pretendin that I don't mind
Oh Davy boy
Why are you blind blind blind?

(Music continues beneath.)

(Enter DAVID.*)*

DAVID/JOSEPH: Agnes! Agnes! You'll never believe
what happened.

AGNES/SIMON: What?

DAVID/JOSEPH: Mister Spenlow told me I could never
marry his daughter!

AGNES/SIMON: Really?!?

DAVID/JOSEPH: Yes. But then he had a heart attack and
died. Isn't that great?!? *(He exits.)*

AGNES/SIMON: Aaaaaaaa! *(She takes a moment to regain
her composure.)*

AGNES/SIMON & GABE:
Oh Davy, Davy
How I wish that you were mine
Oh Davy boy
Why are you blind blind blind?

*(*AGNES *exits dejectedly.)*

(MATTHEW *and* GABE *sing a bridal march—con brio.*)

Song: **Bridal March**

MATTHEW & GABE:

Here comes the bride
Here comes the bride
Here comes the
Here comes the
Here comes the bride

(DAVID *enters dressed as a groom.*)

(ADAM *enters as* DORA *in a bridal gown, carrying a small dog.*)

(GABE *exits.* MATTHEW *takes off his glasses and scarf to reveal his* VICAR *outfit.*)

VICAR/MATTHEW: Do you, David Copperfield, take this woman to be your lawfully wedded wife till death do you part?

DAVID/JOSEPH: I do.

VICAR/MATTHEW: And do you, Dora Spenlow, take...

DORA/ADAM: Oh, the big bad man is scaring me with his serious voice. Woof! Woof! You see? Little Jip is oh so frightened too.

VICAR/MATTHEW: ...do you take this man...

DORA/ADAM: Oh, my little brain is hurting with the big serious words...

VICAR/MATTHEW: ...to be your lawfully wedded husband till death do you part?

DORA/ADAM: Will he buy me lots of pretty hats? And will he give cute little Jip a lovely bone with a pink ribbon?

DAVID/JOSEPH: I will.

DORA/ADAM: He will!

VICAR/MATTHEW: I now pronounce you man and wife.

DORA/ADAM: *(To* DAVID*)* You may now kiss little snookems.

*(*DORA *offers* DAVID *her dog, he kisses it.)*

DORA/ADAM: Oh, I'm so happy!

*(*DORA *happily skips off.* VICAR *exits.)*

DAVID/JOSEPH: *(To audience)* Good lord, what have I done?!? Suddenly it occurs to me that my love for Dora could be the mistaken impulse of an undisciplined heart, and there can be no greater disparity in marriage than unsuitability of mind and purpose.

(Enter AGNES.*)*

AGNES/SIMON: Yo! Davy! You better come check on Dora. She keeps falling down. *(Exit)*

DAVID/JOSEPH: *(To audience)* Thank goodness for her fatal disease. *(Exit)*

(Enter ADAM, *still dressed as a bride, playing an accordion.)*

*(*MATTHEW *enters carrying his train and singing.)*

Song: **Ballad Of Charles Dickens Reprise 3**

MATTHEW:
Charlie Dickens had a wife named Catherine

DICKENS/GABE: *(Spoken)* I married Catherine Hogarth in 1836.

MATTHEW:
She caused him aching in his heart and brain

DICKENS/GABE: *(Spoken)* From the beginning it was an unhappy union, and this influenced my portrayal of David Copperfield's ill-fated marriage to Dora.

MATTHEW: And when he knew that he was sure
That he just couldn't take no more
He saw the shining lights of Drury Lane

(Exit MATTHEW *and* ADAM*)*

(Special on DICKENS.*)*

DICKENS/GABE: "Spare my life for the love of heaven!"
Bill grasped his pistol and beat it twice with all the
force he could summon upon the upturned face
that almost touched his own. She staggered and fell,
nearly blinded with blood. The murderer, staggering
backward to the wall, and shutting out the sight with
his hand, seized a heavy club and struck her down!

(Enter CATHERINE DICKENS *[*SIMON*], from the shadows.
She is carrying a newborn baby.)*

CATHERINE/SIMON: Charles.

DICKENS/GABE: Oh—Catherine. I didn't know you
were there.

CATHERINE/SIMON: What are you doing?

DICKENS/GABE: I'm rehearsing the bludgeoning scene
from Oliver Twist. Don't tell me you've forgotten!

CATHERINE/SIMON: Forgotten what?

DICKENS/GABE: Tomorrow I'm doing my dramatic
reading at Saint James Theatre.

CATHERINE/SIMON: And you're doing the bludgeoning
scene from *Oliver Twist*?

DICKENS/GABE: Yes! Isn't that fantastic?

CATHERINE/SIMON: It's horrible.

DICKENS/GABE: Exactly. It's horrible, but it's
magnificent!

*(*CATHERINE *looks at* DICKENS *sceptically.)*

DICKENS/GABE: Oh, Catherine...I suppose you could
never understand—everything I've done in my life; the
novels, the charity work, the social activism—all of that
is *nothing* compared to the thrill I get from doing this
bludgeoning scene! I just love it!

CATHERINE/SIMON: Charles, don't you want to see your new son?

DICKENS/GABE: New son?!? You mean...you were pregnant?!?

CATHERINE/SIMON: Yes.

DICKENS/GABE: Thank God for that. I thought you were just getting fat. Let's have a look at the lad.

(CATHERINE *shows* DICKENS *the baby.*)

DICKENS/GABE: Ah—he's a handsome boy. Our seventh, child! Lucky number seven!

CATHERINE/SIMON: Tenth, actually.

DICKENS/GABE: Lucky number ten! Let's call him Edward—Edward Bulwer Lytton Dickens!

CATHERINE/SIMON: *(To baby)* Do you hear that, baby? Your daddy says your name is Edward Bulwer Lytton Dickens. *(Beat. To* DICKENS*)* Charles, do you ever feel we don't spend enough time together?

DICKENS/GABE: What do you mean?

CATHERINE/SIMON: I mean, what with the ten kids, and your novels, and your periodical, and the charity work, and the readings...it just seems like we don't have any time left for us.

DICKENS/GABE: *(Produces a letter from his pocket)* Catherine I...I've had a letter.

CATHERINE/SIMON: A letter?

DICKENS/GABE: It's from Wilkie Collins. He's suggested I should become more involved in theatre! And, well you know I've always loved theatre! This could be a new start for me!

CATHERINE/SIMON: A new start is good.

DICKENS/GABE: Yes, a new start. Catherine, you and I...we haven't been good together for a long time. You don't want to have any fun, you're always exhausted, and I need stimulation! I'm sorry, Catherine, I'm sorry to end it like this but I think we should both move on.

CATHERINE/SIMON: Move on?

DICKENS/GABE: I know it sounds hard, but my future is treading the boards, Catherine! The footlights and the roaring crowds! Surrounded by thespians! And your future will be good too, I'll make sure of that. I'll make sure you never want for anything. Catherine? Catherine? ...Please, say something...

CATHERINE/SIMON: I am so sick of your shit.

DICKENS/GABE: What?

CATHERINE/SIMON: I am SO sick of your shit Charles John Huffam Dickens! *(Mimicking him)* "Oh, Catherine, you're tired all the time. You don't wanna have any fun." YOU're the genius who knocked me up ten times—if I'm a little tired that just *might* have something to do with it. Look at me—I'm retaining water, I got piles, this house is lousy with hyperactive children, and you act like it's nothing to do with you! Honestly, I'll be glad to see the back of you, you self-centred dickhead!

DICKENS/GABE: This is most unfair! Have I not been good to you? Have I not given you a good life?!?

CATHERINE/SIMON: How?!? When have you *ever* been good to me?

DICKENS/GABE: Well I...I took you to America, to see the New World!

CATHERINE/SIMON: Oh that turned out to be a barrel of laughs. The Americans hated us—and why? Because you couldn't keep your mouth shut. You had to go and tell them that they should abolish slavery.

DICKENS/GABE: Well they *should* abolish slavery.

CATHERINE/SIMON: What do you care if they have slaves or not!?! Mind your own damn business! We were in Virginia, for God sake.

DICKENS/GABE: Well, if that is how you feel, I guess this separation is for the best!

CATHERINE/SIMON: Darn tootin'!

DICKENS/GABE: Good!

CATHERINE/SIMON: Great!

DICKENS/GABE: Since we seem to be in agreement, this is very straightforward. I won't fight over custody. You can keep the children.

CATHERINE/SIMON: I don't want to keep the damn children. *You* keep the children.

DICKENS/GABE: I can't look after ten kids. You're the mother.

CATHERINE/SIMON: I thought you weren't going to fight over custody.

DICKENS/GABE: I thought you would want to live with your own children.

CATHERINE/SIMON: You thought wrong. These kids are out of control. You want to split up—you keep 'em.

(CATHERINE *shoves the baby into* CHARLES' *arms.*)

DICKENS/GABE: You know children give me anxieties and sorrows.

CATHERINE/SIMON: Oh here we go again with the "anxiety and sorrows".

DICKENS/GABE: But...

CATHERINE/SIMON: Talk to the Ed, because the Catherine Dickens ain't listening.

(CATHERINE *exits one direction,* DICKENS *exits the other.*)

(The lights shift to a warm special on MATTHEW *as he crosses to the easel and produces a new sign.)*

MATTHEW: And now, ladies and gentlemen, we are proud to present that heartbreaking tale of hope deferred—*Great Expectations. (Reveals a new sign reading* GREAT EXPECTATIONS *and exits.)*

(Enter SIMON *carrying a guitar. He ambles across the stage at a leisurely pace, smiling at the audience. When he reaches the sign he takes a look at the card and then launches into the song.)*

Song: **Great Expectations**

SIMON: Pip was an orphan who lived on a marsh
Magwich a convict whose language was harsh
Miss Havisham so wealthy and mean
In a wedding dress that she never got cleaned
Estella was gorgeous, oh yes, she was drop dead
Miss Havisham's daughter, but she was adopted

Well, Pip got rich
He wanted to get hitched
But Stella was a bitch
And Magwich got stitched
Havisham burned
Magwich died
Pip got poor
And time went by
And Estella, so proud and full of hate
Had a change of heart and admitted her fate
It was gettin late as they stood by the gate
She took Pip's hand said "I'll be your mate"
Pip said it was worth the wait
And that's what you get when expectations are great
(He bows, and flips over a sign that reads AND NOW... THE FINAL BIT OF DAVID COPPERFIELD. *He exits.)*

(Lights up on DORA *sitting wrapped in a blanket. She is sick and dying. She still carries her dog.)*

*(*DAVID *kneels by her side.)*

DORA/ADAM: *(In a death swoon)* Oh my dear poopsy.

DAVID/JOSEPH: Yes my love.

DORA/ADAM: I am about to die, but before I leave this world I just want to tell you...

(Knock! Knock! Knock!)

*(*MR PEGGOTTY *enters.)*

MR PEGGOTTY/MATTHEW: *(Overjoyed)* We found her, Mas'r Davy! We found Little Em'ly. She's safe and sound and we're all emigrating to Australia!

DAVID/JOSEPH: That's great news! Really great! Um... could you excuse me for a minute. My wife was just saying her last words.

MR PEGGOTTY/MATTHEW: *(Still overjoyed—oblivious to what* DAVID *just said)* Oh, sure, sure...okay, come see us off on the boat before we leave!

DAVID/JOSEPH: Absolutely.

MR PEGGOTTY/MATTHEW: And bring Dora along.

DAVID/JOSEPH: Oh no, she'll be dead then.

MR PEGGOTTY/MATTHEW: Great, great! Well, I better get back to little Emily.

DAVID/JOSEPH: Yeah, give her my love. *(Back to* DORA*)* Sorry about that, honey. Now what were you saying?

DORA/ADAM: David, my darling, when I am gone I want you to...

(Knock! Knock! Knock!)

(Enter AUNT BETSEY, URIAH HEEP, *and* MR MICAWBER. MR MICAWBER *holds a ledger book in one hand, and is*

fighting off URIAH HEEP *with a straight edge ruler in the other.)*

BETSEY/GABE: Trot! Come here at once and witness this!

HEEP/SIMON: Give me that book!

MICAWBER/MATTHEW: Back you fiend!

DAVID/JOSEPH: Why it's Aunt Betsey, my benevolent benefactor who mysteriously went bankrupt. And she's with Mister Micawber and Uriah Heep. What's up, Aunt Betsey?

BETSEY/GABE: Mister Micawber is exposing Heep for embezzlement and blackmail!

MICAWBER/MATTHEW: I have, in this book, evidence of every penny that this villain has embezzled over the past ten years!

BETSEY/GABE: You see?!? Uriah Heep was pretending to be humble, but actually he was swindling and blackmailing Agnes's father.

HEEP/SIMON: And I would have gotten away with it, too— if it hadn't have been for you meddling kids!

BETSEY/GABE: That means I'm rich again! Mister Micawber, you're a hero! I'm going to send you to Australia!

DAVID/JOSEPH: Three cheers for Mister Micawber!

ALL: Hip hip hooray! Hip hip hooray! Hip hip...

(They are interrupted by a severe coughing fit from DORA.*)*

DORA/ADAM: *(Coughing)* Hack! Hack! Hack!

DAVID/JOSEPH: Oh...I totally forgot. Dora's just about to die.

BETSEY, MICAWBER, & HEEP: Awwww.

DAVID/JOSEPH: Listen, you guys go on ahead and I'll catch up to you later.

BETSEY/GABE: Okay. Bye Trot. Good luck with the fatal disease.

(They exit, leaving DAVID and DORA alone.)

DAVID/JOSEPH: I'm so sorry, my dearest. Now...you were saying?

DORA/ADAM: David, when I'm dead, I want you to marry...aakkk...

(DORA dies. The dog dies.)

(Lights shift to a special on DAVID.)

DAVID/JOSEPH: So there it was...by now I was a famous author, but my wife was dead—and pretty much all my friends who were living were headed across the sea to Australia—the Micawbers, Mister Peggotty, Little Emily. I'll never forget the day I said good-bye to them on that ship...

(GABE, as DICKENS, plays guitar—an atmospheric arpeggio beneath the following speech.)

DAVID/JOSEPH: We found the ship in the river. It was then calm, radiant sunset. Every taper line and spar was visible against the glow. A sight at once so beautiful, so mournful and so hopeful... Mister Peggotty took us below deck. Among the great beams, bulks, and ringbolts of the ship were crowded groups of people, talking, laughing, crying. From babies who had but a week or two of life behind them, to crooked old men and women who seemed to have but a week or two of life before them; and from ploughmen bodily carrying out the soil of England on their boots, to smiths taking away samples of its soot and smoke upon their skins; every age and occupation appeared to be crammed into the narrow compass of the 'tween decks. We said our farewells. The next thing I knew,

I was on the dock, watching that great ship carry my
friends away to their new life across the sea—and I was
left sad and alone.

(Lights shift to GABE.)

Song: **David Copperfield Epilogue**

GABE: For three long years did Davy roam mm hmm
For three long years did Davy roam mm hmm
For three long years did Davy roam
He mourned for his wife then he came home
Mm hmm
Mm hmm
Mm hmm
He took Miss Agnes on his knee mm hmm
he took Miss Agnes on his knee mm hmm

(Everybody enters and joins GABE.)

*(*DORA *is dressed as an angel.)*

ALL: He took Miss Agnes on his knee
And he said Miss Agnes would you marry me
Mm hmm
Mm hmm
Mm hmm
Oh I would gladly be your wife mm hmm
Oh I would gladly be your wife mm hmm
Oh I would gladly be your wife
For I have loved you all my life
Mm hmm
Mm hmm
Mm hmm

(Applause. DORA *reveals a sign that reads*
INTERMISSION.)

(Black out)

END OF ACT ONE

ACT TWO

(Lights up)

(The easel is standing to one side of the stage. A crate, turned up on one side to be used as a stool, stands beside the easel.)

(Enter JOSEPH, MATTHEW *and* SIMON. *They are like excited school kids, talking amongst themselves as they sit down on the floor with their backs to the audience, facing the empty stool.)*

SIMON: *(Quiet but excited)* What do you think it will be?!?

MATTHEW: I don't know.

JOSEPH: Maybe Barnaby Rudge?!?

MATTHEW: Maybe.

SIMON: Shh! Here he comes.

*(*ADAM *enters. He carries a guitar and a sign that is concealed from the audience.)*

*(*ADAM *reaches the easel, pauses for a moment—the boys are waiting eagerly. *ADAM *smiles as he savors the anticipation.)*

*(*ADAM *turns over the sign and places it on the easel.)*

It reads: NICHOLAS NICKLEBY

*(*JOSEPH, MATTHEW *and* SIMON *burst into applause.)*

JOSEPH: Yeah!

SIMON: Alright!

(JOSEPH *and* MATTHEW *high five each other, and then high five* SIMON.)

MATTHEW: Nicholas! I knew it!

JOSEPH: Shhh!

(ADAM *settles onto the stool and starts playing. Throughout, the listeners whoop and throw in excited comments.*)

Song: **Nicholas Nickleby**

ADAM:
There's a young man on the highway
Headed south to Portsmouth town
To see what work an honest man might find
His travelling companion
Is a boy whose name is Smike
A young lad with a simple simple mind
A simple simple mind

(MATTHEW *leaps to his feet, puts his head next to* ADAM's, *and harmonizes with him.*)

ADAM & MATTHEW:
Oh his daddy was a good man
But he died in poverty
Now if you go to Portsmouth
Take a look and you will see
A young man on the highway
His name is Nick'las Nickleby

(JOSEPH *and* SIMON *congratulate* MATTHEW *as he sits back down.*)

ADAM: Do you see him boys

MATTHEW, SIMON & JOSEPH: (*Spoken*) Where?!?

ADAM: Standin' tall and proud
Climbin' up that slope

MATTHEW: (*Spoken*) I see him!

JOSEPH: *(Spoken)* Go Nicholas!

SIMON: *(Spoken)* We love you!

ADAM: And when his pain was unendurable
He met the Brothers Cheeryble
They gave him hope

MATTHEW: *(Spoken)* Damn straight!

JOSEPH AND SIMON: *(Spoken)* Yee haw!

*(MATTHEW whispers something in JOSEPH's ear. JOSEPH
grins, nods, and runs into the wings.)*

ADAM: And now his uncle's lifeless body
Is a-hangin from a rope

*(MATTHEW and SIMON stand on either side of ADAM and
harmonize with him.)*

ADAM, SIMON, MATTHEW: Ahhh ahhh ahhh ahhh

*(JOSEPH runs back in carrying signs like Bob Dylan's in the
black and white film of* Subterranean Homesick Blues.*)*

ALL: Nick-o-las-nick-el-bee
Nick-o-las-nick-el-bee

(JOSEPH displays a sign that reads NICHOLAS. *He drops
it to the floor. He displays a sign that shows a nickel [or a
coin and the symbol for 5 cents]. He drops it to the floor. He
displays a sign that shows a picture of a bee.)*

ALL: Ahhh ahhh ahhh ahhh
Honest brave and practical
Sometimes quite theatrical

(JOSEPH displays a sign that reads HONEST. *He drops it
to the floor. He displays a sign that reads* PRACTICAL. *He
drops it to the floor. He displays a sign that reads* QUITE
THEATRICAL.*)*

ALL: Ahhh ahhh ahhh ahhh
Don't mess with him mister
He's protective of his sister

(On the word "sister", JOSEPH displays a sign that shows a cartoon of Nicholas punching Sir Mulberry Hawk—POW! A cartoon Kate Nicholas looks on, saying MY HERO!)

(JOSEPH, MATTHEW and SIMON sit back down on the floor facing ADAM, as they were at the beginning of the song. They hum along with ADAM in harmony.)

ADAM: He had an evil uncle
Who had a heart of stone
Impervious to pleading, prayers, and tears
He sent young Nick to Yorkshire
To a hellish school belonging to
A villain by the name of Wackford Squeers
The name of Wackford Squeers
(JOSEPH, MATTHEW and SIMON sing along.)

ALL: O then Nicholas got angry
And with strength beyond his years
He thrashed old Wackford soundly
From his ass up to his ears
Then he set all the children free
Our hero Nick'las Nickleby

(JOSEPH, MATTHEW and SIMON turn to face the audience.)

ALL: Then he set all the children free
Our hero Nick'las Nickleby

(Lights shift.)

(All exit except MATTHEW.)

MATTHEW: When Charles Dickens wrote Nicholas Nickleby in 1839, he was a young idealist who thought that he could change the world. It's now twenty-four years later—1863... *(He removes NICHOLAS NICKLEBY from the easel—revealing a sign that reads 1863.)* ...and Dickens has aged beyond his years. He's replaced Catherine with a young actress named Ellen. And his sensational performances of the bludgeoning scene from *Oliver Twist* have left him exhausted and ill. *(He exits.)*

(Lights up on DICKENS, *now an old man. Sitting in bed, staring into oblivion.)*

(Across the stage is a writing desk.)

*(*DICKENS, *seeing that he is alone, tiptoes over to his writing desk. He takes his pen in hand.)*

DICKENS/GABE: *(To pen)* Oh yes, my friend, the time has come once again.

*(*DICKENS *is just about to start writing when* ELLEN *storms in.)*

ELLEN/ADAM: Charles Dickens! What are you doing out of bed?!

DICKENS/GABE: Jeez! Ellen! You gave me a heart attack!

ELLEN/ADAM: You know what the doctor said.

*(*ELLEN *starts dragging* DICKENS *over to the bed.)*

DICKENS/GABE: I'm just going to write for a minute.

ELLEN/ADAM: Oh no you're not. Back to bed! Now!

*(*DICKENS *and* ELLEN *struggle. She wrestles him back to the bed, throwing him down roughly.)*

ELLEN/ADAM: There. Now stay there, old man. Stay there until you're well.

DICKENS/GABE: God, Ellen, I love it when you manhandle me like that. You're so vigorous. Not like my stupid ex-wife.

ELLEN/ADAM: *(Under her breath)* Good one. Mention the ex-wife.

DICKENS/GABE: Ellen! Ellen!

ELLEN/ADAM: *(Exasperated)* What?!

DICKENS/GABE: Look in that box on the desk.

(ELLEN *opens the box and finds a necklace.*)

DICKENS/GABE: That's for you, Ellen.

ELLEN/ADAM: *(Unimpressed)* Thank you Charles. That's sweet. *(She drops the necklace back into the box and heads for the door.)*

DICKENS/GABE: Ellen. Ellen, now look behind that desk. See that thing behind the desk?

(ELLEN *pulls out a painting of* DICKENS *from behind a chair. It's not a very good painting.*)

DICKENS/GABE: That's for you Ellen. It's a painting of me.

ELLEN/ADAM: I can see that.

DICKENS/GABE: Isn't it great? You can look at it and think, "wow, that's him!"

ELLEN/ADAM: You shouldn't have.

(DICKENS *produces a document.*)

DICKENS/GABE: Ellen, Ellen, look at this—it's the deed to a house. I bought you a house Ellen.

ELLEN/ADAM: Charles—

DICKENS/GABE: *(Producing a second document)* I bought one for your mother, too.

ELLEN/ADAM: Charles, enough with the gifts already. You wanna give me a gift? Do what the doctor said and rest. You know why you're in this state, don't you?

DICKENS/GABE: Doctors don't know anything.

ELLEN/ADAM: It's because of that bludgeoning scene from Oliver Twist!

DICKENS/GABE: No, it's because of my fistula.

ELLEN/ADAM: Your fistula?

DICKENS/GABE: That's right.

ELLEN/ADAM: Always with the fistula. What is fistula anyway?

DICKENS/GABE: Believe me, you don't want to know!

ELLEN/ADAM: I do! I do want to know! Every five minutes it's "my fistula this, my fistula that! Oh my aching fistula!" So what IS fistula?

DICKENS/GABE: Look—it's a problem with my ass and that's as far as I'm going.

(There is an uncomfortable pause.)

DICKENS/GABE: Ellen?

ELLEN/ADAM: What.

DICKENS/GABE: Do you find me attractive?

ELLEN/ADAM: Just go to sleep, and we'll talk tomorrow about your problematic ass and how attractive that makes you.

DICKENS/GABE: Seriously, Ellen, have you ever wanted to have children?

ELLEN/ADAM: You mean with you? You're joking, right? *(She starts laughing.)*

DICKENS/GABE: Yes! Of course, it was a joke. I was joking. Ha ha!

(DICKENS joins ELLEN laughing.)

ELLEN/ADAM: *(Really laughing heartily now)* I mean—that would mean we'd have to sleep together! Ha ha!

DICKENS/GABE: Ha! Yeah! That would be outrageous! Ha ha ha! *(His laughter is too much for him and he starts coughing and hyperventilating.)* Uh oh! Uh oh! Not good!

(ELLEN becomes concerned and puts a hand on his forehead.)

ELLEN/ADAM: Oh, you poor baby, you're burning up again. I'll get the flannel. *(Exits)*

(BILL SIKES, carrying his stick/cudgel, enters from the shadows. He is walking a gigantic dog on wheels.)

SIKES/SIMON: *(To dog)* Heel.*(To* DICKENS*)* Hello Charles.

DICKENS/GABE: Bill! Bill Sikes my old friend! I'm so happy to see you!

(ELLEN re-enters with a wet flannel.)

ELLEN/ADAM: Who are you talking to?

DICKENS/GABE: Bill Sikes.

ELLEN/ADAM: There's no-one there, Charles, you're hallucinating.

SIKES/SIMON: Do you want me to club her over the head for you?

DICKENS/GABE: Oh no, no. Don't do that.

ELLEN/ADAM: Don't do what?

DICKENS/GABE: Bludgeon you to death.

ELLEN/ADAM: What the hell are you talking about?!?

(MISS HAVISHAM, in her wedding dress, enters out of the shadows.)

MISS HAVISHAM/JOSEPH: What *are* you talking about, Charles Dickens?!?

SIKES/SIMON: Well well well, if it isn't Miss Havisham.

DICKENS/GABE: *(Holding his head)* Miss Havisham?!? Oh God! I'm losing my marbles!

MISS HAVISHAM/JOSEPH: You look pathetic, Dickens

DICKENS/GABE: Shut up you ugly hag!

ELLEN/ADAM: Charles!

DICKENS/GABE: Not you, Ellen! I'm talking to that other hag. Oh God, how could things get any worse?!?

(Suddenly a man appears from beneath the bed covers. It is MR WARREN with his megaphone.)

MR WARREN/MATTHEW: *(Through megaphone)* Hello Charles!

DICKENS/GABE: Aaaaaaa! *(He hides behind* ELLEN*'s skirt.)* Help me, Ellen. Don't you see them all torturing me?!?

ELLEN/ADAM: Charles, it's just your feverish imagination! Look, there's nobody here. Okay?

*(*DICKENS *takes a good look at* MISS HAVISHAM, MR WARREN, *and* SIKES. *He then turns doubtfully to* ELLEN.*)*

DICKENS/GABE: Um...okay...

*(*ELLEN *tucks* DICKENS *in.)*

ELLEN/ADAM: Now go to sleep.

DICKENS/GABE: Ellen?

ELLEN/ADAM: What.

DICKENS/GABE: Sing me that lullaby?

Song: **Lullabye Dementia**

ELLEN/ADAM:
Lay down my baby
Lay down and take your rest
Lay your head
Upon your mama's breast
You know she loves you
But Jesus loves you the best
Oh m'darlin good night
Good night good night

*(*ELLEN *repeats "oh my darling good night, good night, good night" beneath.)*

MR WARREN/MATTHEW: *(Through megaphone)*
Come back
To the blacking factory *(Repeat)*

MISS HAVISHAM/JOSEPH: With your pen
You made me a jilted bride

Cruel and bitter
Empty inside

DICKENS & SIKES:
I am a man
Of anxiety and sorrow
I am a man
Of anxiety and sorrow *(Repeat)*

(ELLEN reaches the end of her chorus and exits.)

(As soon as she's out the door SIKES bursts into an upbeat riff on the guitar. MATTHEW plays a rhythm on a cabasa.)

(MISS HAVISHAM reaches her hand out to DICKENS.)

MISS HAVISHAM, MR WARREN & SIKES:
La la lala
La la lala
La la lala
La

(DICKENS takes MISS HAVISHAM's hand and they do a lively dance together [jitterbug would be ideal].)

MISS HAVISHAM, MR WARREN & SIKES:
La la lala
La la lala
La la lala
La

DICKENS/GABE:
Welcome to the party that is going on inside my head
Fezziwigs is really rockin'
Mrs Merdle's hair is shockin'
Newman nogs is on the grog
With Wackford squeers now give a cheer
Cuz here comes Scrooge in blue suede shoes
I wish that you were here
Here at the party

(MISS HAVISHAM, MR WARREN and SIKES clap and sing doo-wop beneath.)

DICKENS/GABE:
Inside my head
Here at the party
There's a party goin on inside my head
Oh yeah
Yeah

ALL: Yeah!

(They all join in and build to a screaming chord on the last "yeah".)

(All dance and sing.)

ALL:
La la lala
La la lala
La la lala
La
Oh yeah!
Yeah!
Yeah!

(ELLEN enters and sees DICKENS dancing. She grabs him roughly and pushes him back into bed.)

ALL:
Lay down my baby
Lay down and take your rest
Lay your head
Upon your mama's breast

(MISS HAVISHAM, MR WARREN and SIKES exit, leaving ELLEN with DICKENS who is now asleep.)

ELLEN/ADAM:
You know she loves you
But Jesus loves you the best
Oh m'darlin good night
Good night
Good night

(ELLEN *exits, leaving* DICKENS *alone in his bed. After a beat, he opens his eyes and tip-toes over to his desk. Pen in hand, he begins to write.*)

DICKENS/GABE: It was the best of times, it was the worst of times...

(*A sign is revealed:* A TALE OF TWO CITIES.)

(*Lights up on poor people of France [*ADAM, JOSEPH, MATTHEW, *and* SIMON*]*)

(*Mournful music beneath [played on guitar by* JOSEPH *dressed as* MADAME DEFARGE*], as the peasants speak.*)

PEASANT 1/SIMON: Gosh, it sucks being French and poor.

PEASANT 2/MATTHEW: Yeah, the aristocracy treat us like animals.

PEASANT 3/ADAM: Worse than animals. The other day, I was chewing on an old bone—and this rich guy totally took it away from me and gave it to his dog.

PEASANT 2/MATTHEW: His dog?!? You're shitting me.

PEASANT 3/ADAM: I shit you not. The dude totally took my last old bone.

PEASANT 2/MATTHEW: These really are the worst of times.

PEASANT 1/SIMON: Look out! Here comes a member of the aristocracy driving too fast in his carriage—get that child out of the way!

(*A tricycle carrying a member of the aristocracy [*GABE*] careens onto the stage.*)

(*Lights up on the opposite side of the stage, revealing a rag doll sitting on the floor.*)

ARISTOCRAT/GABE: Aaaaaaaa!

PEASANTS: Aaaaaaaa!

(The tricycle comes to a halt on top of the doll.)

ARISTOCRAT/GABE: Oh great! I'm an aristocrat and I've just run over a small child. If my wheel is bent you guys are in big trouble!

(Father picks up his lifeless child.)

PEASANT 2/MATTHEW: My child! My child is dead! Oh woe is me! Alas!

ARISTOCRAT/GABE: You see, that's why I wasn't going to stop. I knew you were going to make a big deal out of this.

(He notices DEFARGE knitting.)

ARISTOCRAT/GABE: Hey, what's with the knitting? You making a scarf or something? That's not like a coded list of rich people you want to decapitate or anything, is it? None of my business, right? Okay— Listen, I'm outta here. But don't you poor people let your children run under our cart wheels because we're rich, see, and we don't stop for anything. Now scram!!!

(DEFARGE and the PEASANTS scurry off the stage.)

ARISTOCRAT/GABE: Okay, hit it driver, or we'll be late for the chocolate tasting party. *(To audience)* Isn't this a great life: oppressing poor people by day, ambassador's reception at night! These really are the best of times! *Au Revoir!* *(He honks his horn twice and peddles off.)*

(SIMON crosses the stage with a sign that reads MEANWHILE, IN LONDON...)

(Enter CHARLES DARNAY [JOSEPH] and SIDNEY CARTON [ADAM].)

DARNAY/JOSEPH: Hey Sidney Carton.

CARTON/ADAM: Hey Charles Darnay.

(CARTON and DARNAY shake hands.)

DARNAY/JOSEPH: How's it going? You still wallowing in self pity?

CARTON/ADAM: Yeah, and I've got insomnia, and I drink way too much—oh look, here comes Lucie Manette.

(Enter LUCIE *[MATTHEW].)*

DARNAY/JOSEPH: Hi Lucie Manette.

LUCIE/MATTHEW: Hi Charles Darnay and Sidney Carton. Say, did anybody ever tell you guys that you look alike?

CARTON/ADAM: Really?

LUCIE/MATTHEW: Yeah, you guys are like twins. It's amazing. Like, if one of you were in prison, you could switch places and nobody would even know the difference—you're that similar.

CARTON/ADAM: I don't suppose you'd ever want to marry a man like me.

LUCIE/MATTHEW: No, probably not.

CARTON/ADAM: Alright! I'm gonna go get paralytically drunk now.

*(*CARTON *exits.* DR MANETTE *[SIMON] enters carrying a shoemaking workcase.)*

LUCIE/MATTHEW: Hello father.

DR MANETTE/SIMON: Hello my loving daughter.

*(*DR MANETTE *and* LUCIE *kiss each cheek. She exits.)*

DARNAY/JOSEPH: Say, Doctor Manette. What's that thing you got there?

DR MANETTE/SIMON: This? Oh, it's a portable worktable for making shoes. I was locked up in France for eighteen years, I went a little crazy, and I started making shoes. But I'm mostly over it now. I hardly ever make shoes no more.

DARNAY/JOSEPH: Doctor Manette, I'm glad you're here—I want permission to marry your daughter.

DR MANETTE/SIMON: Really!?! Marry my daughter, eh? That is a surprise. (*He opens up his shoe case and begins working on a pair of wooden shoes with a hammer.*)

DARNAY/JOSEPH: I love your daughter fondly, dearly, devotedly. If ever there were love in the world, I love her. You cannot know how earnestly I say it, how earnestly I feel it...Doctor Manette...can you hear me?

(DR MANETTE *has been tapping out a rhythm on the shoes. Now he cuts off* DARNAY *by bursting into song.*)

(ADAM *accompanies on guitar.* GABE *on guitar.* MATTHEW *on wooden fish.*)

Song: **Footsteps**

DR MANETTE/SIMON:
I spent eighteen years in the tower
Eighteen years in hell
You gonna take my little girl
You better take my life as well
I can feel the darkness
Closing in again
Hey there mister
Looks to me
Like you wear size ten

(DR MANETTE *pulls* DARNAY'*s shoe off his foot, knocking him to the ground in the process.*)

DR MANETTE/SIMON:
I hear the times are changing
Revolution's in the air
And I hear footsteps
Footsteps when there aint nobody there

(DR MANETTE *starts hammering madly on* DARNAY'*s shoe.*)

DARNAY/JOSEPH: *(Spoken)* Doctor Manette? Can I have my shoe back?

DR MANETTE/SIMON:
I was an honest doctor
They took away my life
I never knew my baby girl
The sadness killed my wife
Spiralled into madness
Locked in the Bastille

(DR MANETTE offers the shoe back to DARNAY. DARNAY takes it and puts it on.)

DR MANETTE/SIMON:
Now try this on and tell me
If it's tight around the heel
I hear them in the alley
I hear them on the stair
I hear footsteps
Footsteps
When there aint nobody there

ALL:
Hey hey Charles Darnay
Don't you take my little girl away
Hey hey whadda you say
Would you like a pair of those in grey?

DARNAY/JOSEPH: *(Spoken)* I don't want to take your daughter away. I want all three of us to live together and be blissfully happy.

DR MANETTE/SIMON: *(Spoken)* Oh, well that's okay then. *(Sung)*
But I hear those footsteps
Yes I hear footsteps
I hear those footsteps
Don't you hear those footsteps

DARNAY/JOSEPH: I don't hear footsteps

DR MANETTE/SIMON: I hear those footsteps

DARNAY/JOSEPH: There aint no footsteps

DR MANETTE/SIMON: I hear those footsteps
Footsteps
Footsteps
When there aint nobody there

(Music builds to a crescendo as DR MANETTE *does a pathetic riverdance—hop, kick, hop sort of thing, and then bows limply.)*

(End of song. Applause)

(Everyone exits except JOSEPH.*)*

DARNAY/JOSEPH: *(To audience)* It should have been a fairy tale ending: Charles Darnay marries Lucie Manette and they live happily ever after. But it didn't work out that way...

*(*JOSEPH *sets two stools stage right, and a guillotine rolls in from stage left. Beneath the blade is a wicker basket to catch the severed heads in.)*

DARNAY/JOSEPH: ...The French Revolution happened. I tried to help out an old friend, one thing led to another, and I ended up in a prison cell in Paris—sentenced to death.

*(*DARNAY *sits on a stool. Lights shift to make it look like he's in a prison cell.)*

*(*LUCIE *enters.)*

LUCIE/MATTHEW: Oh Charles, my love, how did it come to this!?!

DARNAY/JOSEPH: I'm so sorry, my dearest. Tomorrow I go to the guillotine. Our daughter will grow up without a father.

LUCIE/MATTHEW: Don't lose heart, my love. My father will come to our aid!

DARNAY/JOSEPH: Your father?

LUCIE/MATTHEW: Yes!

DARNAY/JOSEPH: The guy who sings about shoes?

LUCIE/MATTHEW: Yes!

DARNAY/JOSEPH: I'm doomed.

(Enter CARTON.*)*

CARTON/ADAM: Hey Lucy, what's happening?

LUCIE/MATTHEW: Sidney Carton, thank God you're here. Charles is about to get his head chopped off.

CARTON/ADAM: Seriously?

LUCIE/MATTHEW: Yes, seriously.

CARTON/ADAM: That's fantastic! This is my big chance to do something selfless and heroic for a change!

LUCIE/MATTHEW: What are you talking about?!?

CARTON/ADAM: What am I talking about?!? I'll show you—Charles, do you remember how we have an uncommon resemblance?

DARNAY/JOSEPH: Well, I don't really see it.

CARTON/ADAM: Let's exchange hats.

DARNAY/JOSEPH: Okay.

*(*CARTON *and* DARNAY *exchange hats.)*

CARTON/ADAM: Great. Now I'm going to knock you unconscious with this chloroform. Gaoler!

(Enter GAOLER.*)*

GAOLER/GABE: *Oui monsieur?*

*(*CARTON *waves chloroform under* DARNAY's *nose.* DARNAY *falls into the* GAOLER's *arms.)*

CARTON/ADAM: Luckily, by sheer coincidence, this gaoler is a felon from London who owes me a favor, and he's going to help us.

LUCIE/MATTHEW: *(To* GAOLER*)* Is this true?

GAOLER/GABE: Unbelievable, isn't it.

*(*GAOLER *exits dragging off* DARNAY.*)*

CARTON/ADAM: *(To* LUCIE*)* Now, you go back to London, have a kid and name it after me, and I'll just wait here to get my head chopped off. Now go on—off you trot!

LUCIE/MATTHEW: Oh Sidney—you are an angel! How can we ever repay you? Well, see you later. *(She exits.)*

CARTON/ADAM: Great! That worked perfectly. Now let's just hope that nobody recognizes me as an imposter.

*(*DARNAY *sits alone playing a harmonica.)*

(Enter a WOMAN *prisoner.)*

WOMAN/JOSEPH: Excuse me, is this where we wait to get loaded into carts for decapitation?

CARTON/ADAM: Yeah. You getting decapitated today?

WOMAN/JOSEPH: Yeah. I'm a little nervous. This is my first time. How about you?

CARTON/ADAM: Yeah, decapitation for me too. But I'm okay about it.

WOMAN/JOSEPH: Really?

CARTON/ADAM: It feels good to be doing something noble for a change instead of being drunk and debauched.

WOMAN/JOSEPH: Hey—you're Charles Darnay, aren't you?

CARTON/ADAM: Um...yeah...that's right.

WOMAN/JOSEPH: Wait a minute—you're not Charles Darnay! You're just wearing his hat!

CARTON/ADAM: Shhh! Not so loud!

WOMAN/JOSEPH: Oh my God! Are you dying for him?

CARTON/ADAM: And his wife and children.

(Music starts beneath.)

WOMAN/JOSEPH: That is so cool. Brave stranger, I am not unwilling to die, but I am weak and afraid. Will you hold my hand as we ride in the cart?

CARTON/ADAM: Yes, my poor sister, to the last.

(SIMON, still dressed as DR MANETTE, begins strumming a guitar in the background.)

Song: **Far Far Better**

CARTON/ADAM:
The sky has never seemed so blue
And my heart isn't empty any more
It is a far far better thing I do
Than I have ever done before

(GABE as GAOLER joins in on the piano.)

WOMAN/JOSEPH:
Stranger won't you put your hand in mine
The sun's goin' down and the light is dyin'
Let those wagon wheels roll
Hold my hand and don't let go

(Lights up on guillotine. An EXECUTIONER [MATTHEW] stands beside the blade, rope in hand.)

CARTON/ADAM:
Do you see that shining guillotine
That is the sweetest sight I have ever seen
Little sister hold my hand

BOTH:
We're headed for the promised land
Oh the sky has never seemed so blue
My heart isn't empty any more

(EXECUTIONER *leads* WOMAN *to the guillotine and sticks her head beneath the blade.*)

CARTON/ADAM:
It is a far far better thing I do
Than I have ever done before

(*Whack! The blade comes down and chops off the woman's head. Her head flies off and lands in the basket.*)

(*Now it's* CARTON'S *turn. He dances happily to the executioner.*)

(*The others harmonize with angelic "ahhh"s and "oooo"s.*)

CARTON/ADAM:
Oh the sky has never seemed so blue
My heart isn't empty any more
It is a far far better thing I do!!!

(CARTON *sticks his head in the guillotine.*)

(*Chop*)

(*His head falls in the basket.*)

(*The* EXECUTIONER *reaches into the basket and lifts the head out by the hair.*)

(*The head smiles at the audience and sings the final line of the song.*)

CARTON/ADAM:
Than I have ever done before

(*Blackout*)

Song: **Old Curiosity Shop**

(*Lights on* JOSEPH *stage right.*)

JOSEPH: (*Spoken*) Ladies and gentlemen, join us now as we relive the classic tale of a young girl's journey through the bizarre labyrinth of the human psyche— we are proud to present: *The Old Curiosity Shop*

(JOSEPH *reveals a sign reading* THE OLD CURIOSITY SHOP, *and exits.)*

(Enter SIMON, *ambling across the stage with his guitar again. He looks at the sign, looks at the audience, and launches into it.)*

SIMON: Little Nell and her grandfather
Were bothered by a dwarf
So first they travelled west
And then they travelled north
They wound up in a churchyard
Their feet were sore and red
Grandfather was crazy
And little Nell was dead
Thank you.

*(*SIMON *bows and exits. As he goes, he reveals a sign reading:* FOR ONE NIGHT ONLY THE ASTOUNDING MR CHARLES DICKENS.)*

*(*MATTHEW *enters solemnly.)*

MATTHEW: 1870—Saint James Hall, London. Charles Dickens, now old and frail, barely able to walk, performs the murder scene from *Oliver Twist* for the final time. Ladies and Gentlemen—Mister Charles Dickens.

*(*DICKENS *is now an old man with white hair, stooped. He hobbles weakly to center stage. It takes him a moment to steady himself and begin speaking.)*

DICKENS/GABE: Good evening, ladies and gentlemen, it's great to be here. Actually, when you're my age, it's great to be anywhere...heh heh, okay... So here's the moment you've all been waiting for. My world famous bludgeoning scene, from—ah—that book I wrote. The one with the boy in it, and I think there was a dog... with wheels! Okay...here we go... *(He assumes a dramatic posture.)* "Spare my life, for the love of heaven!' The

guy with the hat hit her twice and there was blood,
and then he grabbed a stick or something—no it was
a big, like a club, only bigger. And he was swinging it
and swinging it! Ahh! Ahh! Ahh! No! And there was
even more blood—just loads of it. And WOOOSH!
He burst into flames! YES! And—NO! Wait! That
was *Bleak House*! You know, ladies and gentlemen,
spontaneous human combustion is no joke—they
laughed at me, but believe me—it's very very real.
So—uh, anyway, at this point the red haired lady was
dead, because the guy in the hat had killed her. He had
BLUDGEONED her to death. BLUDGEONED ladies
and gentleman—BLUDGEONED. No need to applaud,
I fully understand your stunned silence. *(He coughs
and grabs his chest.)* Uh oh! Uh oh! Not good! I'm going
home now to lie down for a while...good night, ladies
and gentlemen...good night..

(As DICKENS *sadly totters toward the wings stage right,
the lights shift and* ADAM *begins playing and atmospheric
arpeggio on the guitar.)*

*(*JOSEPH *enters and gently puts his arm around* DICKENS's
shoulder.)

JOSEPH: *(Quietly)* Can I help you?

DICKENS/GABE: No. I'll be fine. *(He exits.)*

*(*JOSEPH *crosses to center stage. He removes his hat and
speaks to the audience.)*

JOSEPH: *(To audience)* The sick man laid his hand upon
his attendant's arm. "Open the window", the sick man
said. He did so. The noise of carriages and carts, the
rattle of wheels, the cries of men and boys floated into
the room. Above the hoarse loud hum, arose from time
to time a boisterous laugh; or a scrap of song would
strike upon the ear for an instant, and then be lost
amidst the roar of voices and the tramp of footsteps.
"There is no air here", said the sick man faintly. He

folded his hands, and murmuring something more they could not hear, fell into a sleep—only a sleep at first, for they saw him smile. He had grown so like death in life, that they knew not when he died. *(He exits.)*

(CATHERINE *places a tombstone that reads* Here Lies Charles Dickens. *She puts a bouquet of flowers in front of it.)*

(ELLEN *enters, also carrying flowers.)*

(CATHERINE *and* ELLEN *freeze when they see each other.)*

ELLEN/ADAM: Catherine.

CATHERINE/SIMON: Ellen.

(CATHERINE *and* ELLEN *hug each other.)*

ELLEN/ADAM: I'm so glad you came.

CATHERINE/SIMON: Me too. How are you bearing up?

ELLEN/ADAM: Okay. I still can't believe he's gone.

CATHERINE/SIMON: Yeah, well it was inevitable wasn't it?

ELLEN/ADAM: It was that stupid bludgeoning scene from *Oliver Twist*, that's what killed him

CATHERINE/SIMON: I know. Every time I picked up a newspaper it was the same story— "Charles Dickens thrills audience with murder scene from *Oliver Twist*." And they kept rushing him to hospital because he was knocking himself senseless.

ELLEN/ADAM: I tried to stop him, but would he listen?

CATHERINE/SIMON: Him?!? listen?! Oh please!

ELLEN/ADAM: He just loved doing that bludgeoning scene.

CATHERINE/SIMON: God he was weird. I still loved him though.

ELLEN/ADAM: Me too. (*She puts her flowers on the grave.*)

(*In the shadows upstage,* DICKENS *is playing an arpeggio on his guitar.*)

Song: **Grave**

ELLEN/ADAM:
Farewell now Charles Dickens
It's time to say good-bye

(MR WARREN *appears out of the shadows. He places flowers on the grave.*)

MR WARREN/MATTHEW:
We will meet again some day
In that great blacking fact'ry in the sky

CATHERINE/SIMON:
I loved you so, you were my heart's desire

(*Enter* MISS HAVISHAM.)

MISS HAVISHAM/JOSEPH:
I loved you even though you set me on fire

ALL:
You'll never walk these streets again
Or catch the dreams you once pursued
We'll never know the ending of
The Mystery of Edwin Drood
Things will never be the same
[Charlie Dickens walked the streets of London town]
He walked the streets of London town

CATHERINE/SIMON:
Charlie Dickens had a wife named Catherine

MR WARREN/MATTHEW:
He never came back to the factory

ELLEN/ADAM:
He used to call me Nell

ALL: Things will never be the same
[Charlie Dickens walked the streets of London town]
He walked the streets of London town

(DICKENS, MISS HAVISHAM, *and* MR WARREN *exit.*)

(ELLEN *begins to sob.*)

CATHERINE/SIMON: Oh...now now, don't cry.

ELLEN/ADAM: I don't want him to be dead. What if people forget about him?

CATHERINE/SIMON: They won't forget. People will remember—maybe not him, but his stories.

ELLEN/ADAM: His stories?

CATHERINE/SIMON: Yes.

ELLEN/ADAM: Like *Martin Chuzzlewit*?

CATHERINE/SIMON: No, not that one. But there is one story of his that I think will be remembered.

(CATHERINE *and* ELLEN *exit.*)

(MATTHEW *rings jingly bells.* JOSEPH *plays the first few notes of Jingle Bells on the ukulele. They bow.*)

(DICKENS *crosses with a sign reading* A CHRISTMAS CAROL.)

(*JOSPEH exits.*)

(MATTHEW *is alone on stage.*)

MATTHEW: *(To audience)* Marley was dead to begin with. There was no doubt about that. Scrooge had never taken his name off the business: Scrooge and Marley.
Scrooge was a tight-fisted hand at the grindstone: a squeezing, wrenching, grasping, scraping, clutching, covetous, old sinner!

(Lights up on SCROOGE *and* BOB CRATCHIT. SCROOGE *paces looking over the shoulder of Bob Cratchit who sits nervously at a stool, writing in a ledger book.)*

MATTHEW: Once upon a time on Christmas Eve—old Scrooge and his poor clerk Bob Cratchit sat busy in his counting-house. It was cold, bleak, biting weather, when Scrooge's nephew entered.

*(*MATTHEW *steps into the scene, ringing the bell on the door as he approaches* BOB *and* SCROOGE.*)*

NEPHEW/MATTHEW: A merry Christmas, Uncle! God save you!

SCROOGE/ADAM: Bah! Humbug! Every idiot who goes about with "Merry Christmas" on his lips, should be boiled with his own pudding, and buried with a stake of holly through his heart!

NEPHEW/MATTHEW: Come, Uncle, dine with us tomorrow.

SCROOGE/ADAM: I'll see you in Hell first. Good afternoon.

*(*NEPHEW *exits.)*

(A GENTLEMAN *enters, carrying a book and a pen. He rings the bell on the door as he approaches.)*

GENTLEMAN/SIMON: Scrooge and Marley's, I believe. Have I the pleasure of addressing Mister Scrooge or Mister Marley?

SCROOGE/ADAM: Mister Marley died—seven years ago, this very night.

GENTLEMAN/SIMON: At this festive season of the year, Mister Scrooge, it is more than usually desirable that we should make some slight provision for the poor and destitute. What shall I put you down for?

SCROOGE/ADAM: Nothing! I don't make merry myself at Christmas and I can't afford to make idle people merry. Workhouses are costly enough; and those who are badly off must go there.

GENTLEMAN/SIMON: Many can't go there and would rather die.

SCROOGE/ADAM: If they would rather die, they had better do it, and decrease the surplus population. *(He changes into his night dress as he speaks.)*

GENTLEMAN/SIMON: Well! *(He exits.)*

SCROOGE/ADAM: And you, Cratchit—

BOB/JOSEPH: Yes sir?

SCROOGE/ADAM: You'll want all day off tomorrow, I suppose?

BOB/JOSEPH: If quite convenient, sir.

SCROOGE/ADAM: It's not convenient. Be here all the earlier next morning. Good night.

(BOB scurries away.)

SCROOGE/ADAM: Merry Christmas...bah humbug!

(Enter ghost of MARLEY, draped in chains.)

MARLEY/MATTHEW: Oooooo!

SCROOGE/ADAM: *(Jumping back)* Aaaa! Who are you?

MARLEY/MATTHEW: In life I was your partner, Jacob Marley.

SCROOGE/ADAM: I don't believe you.

MARLEY/MATTHEW: Why do you doubt your senses?

SCROOGE/ADAM: I ate a microwave burrito earlier and I think I might be hallucinating. *(Note: substitute name of an alternative potentially toxic food if there is a local reference that will get a big laugh.)*

MARLEY/MATTHEW: I wear the chain I forged in life, I made it link by link, and of my own free will I wore it. I am here to warn you that you have yet a chance of escaping my fate. You will be haunted by three spirits. Expect the first when the bell tolls one. *(He exits.)*

(A bell rings.)

(The GHOST OF CHRISTMAS PAST *enters. He has a white robe, a huge white long haired wig and a long white beard, and he is carrying a large photo album.)*

SCROOGE/ADAM: Aaa! Who and what are you?!?

PAST/JOSEPH: I am the Ghost of Christmas Past. Come, look in my photo album.

*(*PAST *opens his photo album so that* SCROOGE *can take a look.)*

SCROOGE/ADAM: *(Looking at book)* Oh look, that's me as a little boy at school. At Christmas I was friendless and sad. And that's me as a young man, working for jolly old Fezziwig. He and his wife sure knew how to celebrate Christmas. And look, here's my fiance who deserted me because I loved money more than I loved her. Thanks, Spirit, you taught me a good lesson.

PAST/JOSEPH: Bye.

SCROOGE/ADAM: Bye.

*(*PAST *exits.)*

(The bell rings twice.)

(The GHOST OF CHRISTMAS PRESENT *enters. He rolls in kneeling on a skateboard. He wears a long robe and vegetation on his head.)*

PRESENT/MATTHEW: Oooooo!

SCROOGE/ADAM: You must be the Ghost of Christmas Present.

PRESENT/MATTHEW: Yes I am.

SCROOGE/ADAM: What have you got for me?

PRESENT/MATTHEW: Well, I thought I'd take you to Bob Cratchit's house.

SCROOGE/ADAM: You mean my poor clerk who I treat very badly?

PRESENT/MATTHEW: That's the one. I thought it would be good for you to see that he has a really lovely Christmas even though he's poor.

SCROOGE/ADAM: Really?

PRESENT/MATTHEW: Yes. And did you know he has a crippled son?

SCROOGE/ADAM: I did not know that.

PRESENT/MATTHEW: Here he comes now.

(Lights shift to reveal a small stool.)

(BOB is gently helping TINY TIM [SIMON] who walks with the aid of a crude wooden crutch.)

BOB/JOSEPH: Here you go, Tiny Tim. Sit on this stool beside the fire.

(TINY TIM sits on the stool, as BOB greets his wife [GABE].)

WIFE/GABE: Merry Christmas, my darling husband.

BOB/JOSEPH: And a happy New Year, my devoted wife.

WIFE/GABE: How was Tiny Tim?

BOB/JOSEPH: As good as gold. At church he said he hoped people would see that he was a cripple so they would remember who made the blind man walk.

WIFE/GABE: You really love that boy, don't you.

BOB/JOSEPH: Let me tell you in a song...

(WIFE produces a guitar and begins playing.)

Song: **Tiny Tim**

BOB/JOSEPH:
His bones are weak and brittle
His eyes are pale and dim
He has a twisted foot
And withered limbs
But I will be there when he needs me
Hold his little hand in mine
He is my darling boy
My heart belongs to him
He's Tiny Tim
Oh Tiny Tim

(PRESENT *begins shaking a percussion instrument [e.g. a plastic egg filled with sand] in time with the music.*)

(PRESENT, SCROOGE *and* WIFE *harmonize with "ooo"s and "ahhh"s.*)

BOB/JOSEPH:
On Christmas eve I watch him sit beside the fire
He is so frail I am afraid he will expire
So I do all I can to help my crippled son
Because I love to hear his voice cry out
God bless us every one!

(*The music reaches a crescendo.*)

(*There is an electric guitar built into* TINY TIM'*s wooden crutch. He launches into a fiery electric guitar solo. The solo builds to a manic frenzy complete with screeching feedback. He kicks over his stool and is about to smash his guitar when he's restrained by* BOB. *Once* TINY TIM *settled back on his stool,* BOB *resumes singing.*)

BOB/JOSEPH:
And now the snow is falling

(*A shower of snow falls on* BOB'*s head.*)

BOB/JOSEPH:
I smile and thank the Lord

And pray for just one Christmas more
That I can spend with him
With Tiny Tim
Oh Tiny Tim

(The CRATCHIT *family [*BOB, TINY TIM, *and* WIFE*] exit.)*

SCROOGE/ADAM: Spirit, that boy rocks! Tell me if Tiny Tim will live.

PRESENT/MATTHEW: I see a vacant seat in the poor chimney-corner, and a crutch without an owner, carefully preserved. If these shadows remain unaltered by the future, the child will die. What then? If he be like to die, he had better do it, and decrease the surplus population. Good-bye Scrooge.

*(*PRESENT *turns to leave. As he turns we see the back of his robe for the first time—it is embroidered with the words* TINY TIM WORLD TOUR—1843*)*

PRESENT/MATTHEW: Don't say I didn't warn you. *(He rolls into the wings on his skateboard.)*

(The bell rings three times.)

(Enter SIMON *the* GHOST OF CHRISTMAS YET TO COME.*)*

FUTURE/SIMON: Wooooo!

SCROOGE/ADAM: Are you the Ghost of Christmas Yet to Come?

FUTURE/SIMON: Yup.

SCROOGE/ADAM: Okay, let's see what you've got... *(Looking into the distance)* ...aaa! What's that horrible thing? Down there, next to the Thames!

FUTURE/SIMON: That's the Millennium Dome.

SCROOGE/ADAM: What kind of idiot would build a Millennium Dome?!? It's hideous!

FUTURE/SIMON: That's nothing. Gaze into the box of terror.

*(Three figures [*GABE, JOSEPH, *and* MATTHEW*] sweep in and push* SCROOGE *into a chair facing a television.)*

*(*FUTURE *points a remote at the T V.)*

FUTURE/SIMON: Click.

*(*SCROOGE *is illuminated by a bright light coming from the T V.)*

NEWSCASTER/GABE: *(Ultra-dramatic)* This has been News 34. Recapping our headlines: it's war in the Middle East; the polar icecaps continue to melt; and bird flu has claimed the last surviving turkey—there'll be no holiday dinner this year. Coming up next— *(As if this is the most horrible thing yet)* —it's the Vicar of Dibley Christmas Special!!! *(Or substitute name of lamest Christmas television special)*

*(*SCROOGE *screams in terror and leaps from his seat.)*

SCROOGE/ADAM: God no! Spirit, what is this box!?

FUTURE/SIMON: It's called a television. It shows you what the future of Christmas will be.

SCROOGE/ADAM: Please, spirit, can it tell me if Tiny Tim will live?

*(*FUTURE *points his remote at the T V again.)*

FUTURE/SIMON: Click.

ANNOUNCER/MATTHEW: We now return to our classic Christmas drama: The Night Tiny Tim Died.

SCROOGE/ADAM: Doh!!

*(*SCROOGE *watches the drama unfold on the television, as* JOSEPH *and* GABE *provide the voices.)*

BOB/JOSEPH: I still can't believe that my little angel is gone.

WIFE/GABE: Bob, you've got to move on. Let him go.

BOB/JOSEPH: I can't...Christmas isn't Christmas without Tiny Tim.

WIFE/GABE: He's been dead for a year now. Shouldn't we at least bury him?

SCROOGE/ADAM: Nooooo!

(SCROOGE *closes his eyes as he screams.* GABE, JOSEPH, MATTHEW, *and* SIMON *laugh madly and exit, taking the television and stool with them.*)

(*When* SCROOGE*e opens his eyes he is alone. In a panic he tries to recap what happened to him.*)

SCROOGE/ADAM: Oh my God! There was a ghost! And he had a photo album! And a skate board! The boy had an electric guitar! Good lord! There was a television! (*Looks around and realizes that things are back to normal.*) Oh...I'm back in Victorian London! There's the debtors prison! And the poorhouse! (*Takes a deep breath*) I can smell the raw sewage wafting from the Thames! Thank God I'm home. Merry Christmas everybody!

(BOB *enters with* TINY TIM.)

SCROOGE/ADAM:Bob Cratchit?!?

BOB/JOSEPH: (*Flinching*) Yes sir?

SCROOGE/ADAM: Just the man I wanted to see. Do you know what I'm going to do to you?!?

BOB/JOSEPH: What, sir?

SCROOGE/ADAM: I'm going to double your salary! And I'm going to be a second father to Tiny Tim, who is *not* going to die!

TINY TIM/SIMON: Yeah!

SCROOGE/ADAM: And I'm going to join you for a Christmas feast!

BOB/JOSEPH: Are you on drugs?

SCROOGE/ADAM: No, Bob, no...I've seen the light. The light in the eyes of a child.

Song: **Tiny Tim Reprise**

SCROOGE/ADAM:
I thought that Christmas day was bogus

ALL:
Bogus

SCROOGE/ADAM:
A holiday for fools

ALL:
Fools

SCROOGE/ADAM:
So I was miserly and cruel
I thought that being stingy was cool—ow!
(He starts dancing.)
But then some ghosts taught me a lesson

ALL:
Ooo, scary

SCROOGE/ADAM:
Showed me how my life was grim

ALL: Grim

SCROOGE/ADAM:
I saw a boy who filled my heart
Right up to the brim

BOB/JOSEPH: *(Spoken)* Tiny Tim?

SCROOGE/ADAM: *(Spoken)* Oh yes.

BOTH:
Tiny Tim

(They all start dancing a box step—even TINY TIM, who stuggles with the footwork.)

ALL:
Oh Tiny Tim
Ohhhhhh!!!

TINY TIM/SIMON: Merry Christmas everybody. And
God bless us, every one! *(He plays a power chord.)*

(SCROOGE and the others rock out.)

(Everyone leaps in the air as the song ends.)

(Black out)

(Lights up on SIMON playing guitar.)

(Enter GABE.)

*(Throughout the song, the other actors enter and place signs
around the stage bearing the titles of DICKENS's works.)*

Song: **Finale**

GABE:
These were the works of Charles Dickens
A treasure of prose both timeless and rare
Fiction and fact of exceptional power
A canon of genius beyond compare

MATTHEW & JOSEPH:
The glory of *Message From The Sea*
The magical *Tale of Two Cities*

ADAM & GABE
We liked *Hard Times* we loved *The Chimes*
We dote upon *Nicholas Nickleby*

SIMON:
Dombey and Son was hard to top
But so was *Curiosity Shop*

ADAM:
Pardon me boys
Don't mean to be rude
But don't forget *Mystery of Edwin Drood*

JOSEPH:
Charlie walked beneath coal black skies
Told us stories that opened our eyes

GABE:
He painted a world
In all of his works
Where beadles were evil
And judges were jerks

MATTHEW:
Charlie hated hypocrisy
He yearned for love and humanity

SIMON: *Dorrit* and *Romance* and *Idle Apprentice*
Our Mutual Friend Pickwick Papers and *Mudfog*
The Battle of Life and *American Notes*

OTHERS: *(Building beneath* SIMON*)*
Charlie Charlie Charlie

ALL: Charlie
Charlie
Charlie
Charlie
Charlie
Char—lee— Dick—kens

MATTHEW:
Charlie Dickens walked the streets of London town
He wandered through the smoke from west to east
And only when he finally lay
His bones six feet beneath the clay
Did Charlie Dickens' troubled soul find peace

ALL: Lay down Charles Dickens
Lay down and take your rest
Lay your head
Upon your saviour's breast
You know we love you
But Jesus loves you the best

And we bid you
Good night
Good night
Good night
And we bid you
Good night [good night]
Good night [good night]
Good night [good night]

JOSEPH: I see you walkin' cross the Hungerford Bridge

ALL: And we bid you
Good night [good night]
Good night [good night]
Good night [good night]

JOSEPH: You rob from the rich and you give to the poor

ALL: And we bid you
Good night [good night]
Good night [good night]
Good night [good night]

JOSEPH: Reminding me a little of Simon Cowell

ALL: And we bid you
Good night [good night]
Good night [good night]
Good night

JOSEPH: Goodbye, Charles Dickens.

END OF PLAY

.

www.ingramcontent.com/pod-product-compliance
Lightning Source LLC
Chambersburg PA
CBHW052205090426
42741CB00010B/2412